How to Get Rid of "it"

Before "it" Gets Rid of You

Topical Handbook for
Healing and Deliverance Through
Spiritual Warfare

A Practical Self-Help Guide to
Spiritual and Personal Growth

A series of easy spiritual exercises, interactive tools,
And step-by-step instructions to receive
Freedom from bondage
And experience spiritual healing and deliverance

Volume Five

ISBN-13: 978-1986306461

ISBN-10: 1986306461

How to Get Rid of "it"

Before "it" Gets Rid of You

Topical Handbook for
Healing and Deliverance Through
Spiritual Warfare

A Practical Self-Help Guide to
Spiritual and Personal Growth

A series of easy spiritual exercises, interactive tools,
And step-by-step instructions to receive
Freedom from bondage
And experience spiritual healing and deliverance

Volume Five

Compilations of Works
By
Dr. Paulette Douglas

DEDICATION

**This book is dedicated to my Loving, Supportive, Faithful Father,
The Late Mr. Melvin J. Woods Sr.**

**All my life my Father has inspired me to be the Women that God has ordained me to be
and continue to minister to God's people and to make full proof of my ministry**

CONTENT

How to Get Rid of "it", Before "it" Gets Rid of You

PREFACE

How to Get Rid of "it", Before "it" Gets Rid of You is a Deliverance and Spiritual Warfare Manual compiled by Dr. Paulette Douglas which is worth reading and re-reading more than once, in order to empower the reader when confronting personal crisis and trials. Dr. Paulette Douglas has compiled many practical, spiritual books bringing light to the evil that exists. She brings the deliverance ministry to the forefront, explaining how each and every believer can counteract evil and the devil. Not many believers understand the concept of the Holy Spirit and that we are all called to fight against the devil, our enemy. Dr. Paulette Douglas presents scriptural background and Bible passages from the old and new testaments, as well as prayers to share with the reader that each of us is called to resist and fight against the devil with the power of the Holy Spirit. Dr. Paulette Douglas refers to this as the deliverance ministry and explains this is one of the privileges all believers have at our disposal.

This background scripture material is necessary as many readers may be unfamiliar with these spiritual concepts. The main focus on the book is to be a manual; or one stop guide to show the reader what the bible has to say about deliverance as well as to expose the works and deceptions of the devil as well. The cover itself might seem an actual handbook- yet this book is truly a manual for deliverance. This exhaustive book contains too much information to be digested in a single, quick reading. The words contained are life changing. While some traditional readers and those in organized religion may find this book difficult to believe and a bit theatrical, a close-minded attitude is exactly what the devil wants in order to operate.

It is important to keep in mind the charismatic background of Dr. Paulette Douglas is based on the belief of the real workings of the Holy Spirit and the literal belief in modern day spiritual gifts such as tongues and healing. Much of the book is an invaluable resource where Dr. Douglas has taken scriptural truths and prayers and relates them to the modern-day believer to use and apply when facing any trial or work from the enemy. The scriptural references will empower any reader with a quick resource of how to respond in faith to any difficulty- large and small. It is a spiritual self-help book in the fact that it will allow the reader the tools to look within himself/her-self and identify any areas or issues where Satan has his foothold. Not only that it tells the reader how to face and address these issues! For those who are at a loss of how to begin to approach their spiritual problems there are a number of sample prayers applicable to any number of situations. The reader will get the impression as if this book was written for his or her own situation. This is a book to meditate on and use- and is not intended to collect dust on a book shelf. There are eleven sequels to this handbook which address many other issues that just might cover your "it".

In this twelve-book series, How to Get Rid of "it" Before "it" gets Rid of You we discuss evil spirits and how they operate:
1. The Apostolic anointing and ministry
2. How demons enter and oppress people
3. Curses and how to deal with them
4. Breaking bondages
5. Casting out spirits
6. Healing the wounded heart

7. Ungodly beliefs
8. Ministering to people
9. House cleansing
10. Discerning of spirits

In this volume, we deal with the root causes of the "it' of spiritual warfare and How to get rid of the "it" of spiritual warfare before it gets rid of you. Spiritual warfare is something what plagues many people today, whether addiction to food, sex, drugs, alcohol, smoking, spending, masturbation, porn, etc. Some inexperienced deliverance ministers might go after a spirit of warfare, which may bring freedom, but often, it doesn't bring lasting freedom. Many times, there is a root that needs to be pulled up, alongside casting out any residing spirits that are holding the person in bondage. Getting to the root of the spiritual warfare is the key to bringing a person lasting genuine freedom. I am going to address the most common roots to spiritual warfare, and hopefully give you an idea of how this bondage works so that you can minister lasting freedom to this type of bondage.

INTRODUCTION

"It Is Finished"
The Words of Victory

"When Jesus therefore had received the vinegar, he said, "It is finished.""—John 19:30
Words of triumph. In His words, "My God, my God, why hast thou forsaken me?" we heard the
Savior's cry of desolation. In His words, "I thirst" we listened to His cry of lamentation. Now
there falls upon our ears His cry of jubilation— "It is finished." From the words of the victim we
turn now to the words of the Victor. The Cross of Christ has two great sides to it: it showed the
profound depths of His humiliation, but it also marked the goal of the Incarnation, and further, it
told the consummation of His mission, and it forms the basis of our salvation.

It is finished." What is found in these three words, "It is finished" is wrapped up the Gospel of
God. In these words, contained the ground of the believer's assurance. In those words, is
discovered the sum of all joy, and the very spirit of all divine consolation. Every" it" that we
could ever encounter in our lives was dealt with on the cross therefore; we have the victory
through Jesus Christ over any and every "it".

"It is finished." This was not the despairing cry of a helpless martyr. It was not an expression of
satisfaction that the termination of His sufferings was now reached. It was not the last gasp of a
worn-out life. No, rather was it the declaration on the part of the divine Redeemer that all for
which He came from heaven to earth to do, was now done; that all that was needed to reveal the
full character of God had now been accomplished; that all that was required by the Law before
sinners could be saved, had now been performed—that the full price of our redemption was now
paid.

"It is finished." The great purpose of God in the history of man was now accomplished—from
the beginning, God's purpose has always been one and indivisible. It had been declared to men
in numerous ways: in symbol and type, by mysterious hints and by plain intimations, through
Messianic prediction and through didactic declaration. That purpose of God may be summarized
thus: to display His grace in the creating of children in His own image and glory. And at the
Cross the foundation was laid which was to make this possible and actual.

"It is finished." What was finished? The answer to this question is a very full one, though many
excellent expositors have sought to limit the scope of these words and to confine them strictly to
a single application. We are told it was the prophecies concerning the sufferings of Jesus which
were finished, and that He referred only to this. It is readily granted that the immediate reference
was to the Messianic predictions, yet we think there are good and sufficient reasons for not
confining our Lord's words here to them. Yea, to us it seems certain that Christ referred specially
to His sacrificial work, for all Scripture concerning His suffering and shame was not yet fulfilled.
There remained the dismissal of His spirit into the hands of the Father (Psa 31:5); there remained
the "piercing" with the spear (Zec 12:10: and note that the word used in Psalm 22:16 for the
piercing of His hands and feet—the act of crucifixion—is a different one); there still remained
the preserving of His bones unbroken (Psa 34:20), and the burial in the rich man's grave (Isa
53:9).

"It is finished." What was finished? We answer His sacrificial work. It is true there yet remained the act of death itself, which was necessary for the making of atonement. But, as is so often the case here in John's Gospel wherein our text is found (cf. Joh 12:23, 31; 13:31; 16:5; 17:4), the Lord here speaks of the completion of His work. Moreover, it must be remembered that the three hours darkness was already past, the awful cup had already been drained, His precious blood had already been shed, the outpoured wrath of God had already been endured; and these are the primary elements in the making of propitiation. The sacrificial work of Jesus, then, was completed, excepting only the act of death which followed immediately. But, as we shall see, the completing of the sacrificial work made an end of several things.

"It is finished."
1. Here we see the accomplished fulfillment of all the prophecies which had been written of Him here He should die. This is the immediate thought of the context: "When Jesus therefore had received the vinegar, He said, It is finished" (John 19:30). Centuries beforehand, the prophets of God had described step by step the humiliation and suffering which the coming Savior should undergo. One by one these had been fulfilled, wonderfully fulfilled, fulfilled to the very letter. Had prophecy declared that He should be the "woman's seed" (Gen 3:15), then He was "born of a woman" (Gal 4:4). Had prophecy announced that His mother should be a "virgin" (Isa 7:14), then was it literally fulfilled (Mat 1:18). Had prophecy revealed that He should be of the seed of Abraham (Gen 22:18), then mark its fulfillment (Mat 1:1). Had prophecy made it known that He

Prophecy said that He should be named before He was born (Isa 49:1), then so it came to pass (Luke 1:30-31). Had prophecy foretold that He should be born in Bethlehem of Judea (Mic 5:2), then mark how this very village was His birthplace. Had prophecy forewarned that His birth should entail sorrowing for others (Jer 31:15), then behold its tragic fulfillment (Mat 2:14-18). Had prophecy foreshown that the Messiah should appear before the scepter of tribal ascendancy had departed from Judah (Gen 49:10), then so He did, for though the ten tribes were in captivity, Judah was still in the land at the time of His advent. Had prophecy referred to the flight into Egypt and the subsequent return into Palestine, (Hose 11:1 and cf. Isa 49:3, 6), then so it came to pass (Mat 2:1415).

Prophecy made mention of one going before Christ to make ready His way (Mal 3:1), then see its fulfillment in the person of John the Baptist. Had prophecy made it known that at the Messiah's appearing "the eyes of the blind shall be opened, and the ears of the deaf shall be unstopped, then shall the lame man leap as a hart, and the tongue of the dumb sing" (Isa 35:56), then read through the four Gospels and see how blessedly this proved true. Had prophecy spoken of Him as "poor and needy" (Psa 40:17, see beginning of Psalm), then behold Him not having where to lay His head. Had prophecy intimated that He should speak in "parables" (Psa 78:2), then such was frequently His method of teaching. Had prophecy depicted Him stilling the tempest (Psa 107:29), then this is exactly what He did. Had prophecy heralded His "triumphal entry" into Jerusalem (Zec 9:9), then so it came to pass!

Prophecy announced that His person should be despised (Isa 53:3), that He should be rejected by the Jews (Isa 8:14), that He should be "hated without a cause" (Psa 69:4), then sad to say, such was precisely the case. Had prophecy painted the whole picture of His degradation and crucifixion, then was it vividly reproduced. There had been the betrayal by a familiar friend, the forsaking by His disciples, the being led to the slaughter, the being taken to judgment, the appearing of false witnesses against Him, the refusal on His part to make defense, the establishing of His innocence, the unjust condemnation, the sentence of capital punishment passed upon Him, the literal piercing of His hands and feet, the being numbered with transgressors, the mockery of the crowd, the casting lots for His garments—all predicted centuries beforehand, and all fulfilled to the very letter. The last prophecy of all which remained here He committed His Spirit into the hands of His Father, had now been fulfilled. He cried "I thirst," and after the tendering of the vinegar and gall, all was now "accomplished"; and as the Lord Jesus reviewed the entire scope of the prophetic Word and saw its full realization, He cried,

"It is finished"!
It only remains for us to point out that as there was a complete set of prophecies which had to do with the first advent of Jesus, so also is there a complete set of prophecies which have to do with His second advent—the latter as definite, as personal, and as comprehensive in their scope as the former. As then we see the actual fulfillment of those which had to do with His first coming to the earth, we may look forward with absolute confidence and assurance to the fulfillment of those which have to do with His second coming. And, as we have seen that the former set of prophecies were fulfilled literally and personally, so also must we expect the latter set to be. To grant the literal fulfillment of the former, and then to seek to spiritualize and symbolize the latter, is not only grossly inconsistent and illogical, but is highly injurious to us and deeply dishonoring to God and to His Word.

"It is finished."
2. Here we see the completion of His sufferings. But what tongue or pen can describe the sufferings of Jesus? The anguish, physical, mental, and spiritual, which He endured! Appropriately was He designated "the man of sorrows": suffering at the hands of men, at the hands of Satan, and at the hands of God. Pain inflicted upon Him by enemies and friends alike. From the beginning He walked the shadows which the Cross cast His path. "I am afflicted and ready to die from my youth up" (Psa 88:15). What a light this throws on His earlier years! Who can say how much is contained in those words? For us, an impenetrable veil is cast over the future; none of us knows what a day may bring forth.

But Jesus knew the end from the beginning! One has only to read through the Gospels to learn how the awful Cross was ever before Him. At the marriage-feast of Cana, where all was gladness and merriment, He makes solemn reference to "his hour" not yet come. When Nicodemus interviewed Him at night, the Savior referred to the "lifting up of the Son of man." When James and John came to request from Him the two places of honor in His coming kingdom, He made mention of the "cup" which He had to drink, and of the "baptism" wherewith He must be baptized. When Peter confessed that He was the Christ, the Son of the living God, He turned to His disciples and began to show unto them "how that he must go unto Jerusalem, and suffer many things of the elders and chief priests and scribes, and be killed, and be raised again the third day" (Mat 16:21). When Moses and Elijah stood with Him on the Mount of Transfiguration, it was to speak of "his decease which he should accomplish at Jerusalem" (Luke 9:31).

If it is true we are quite unable to estimate the sufferings of Christ due to the anticipation of the Cross, still less can we fathom the dread reality itself. The physical sufferings were excruciating, but even this was as nothing compared with His anguish of soul. To a consideration of these sufferings we have already devoted several paragraphs in previous chapters, yet we make no apology in turning to them again. We cannot contemplate too often what Jesus endured to secure our salvation. The better we are acquainted with His sufferings, and the more frequently we meditate thereon, the warmer will be our love and the deeper our gratitude.
At last the closing hours have come. There had been the terrible experience in Gethsemane followed by the appearing before Caiaphas, before Pilate, before Herod, and back again before Pilate. There had been the scourging and mocking by the brutal soldiers; the journey to Calvary; the fastening of His hands and feet to the cruel tree. There had been the reviling of the priests, the crowd, and the two thieves crucified with Him.

There had been the awful cloud that hid from the Father's face, which wrung from Him the bitter cry, "My God, my God, why hast thou forsaken me?" There had been the parched lips which drew from Him the exclamation "I thirst." There had been the fearful conflict with the power of darkness as the serpent "bruised" His heel. But now the suffering is ended. The Lord has bruised Him; man, and Devil have done their worst. The cup has been drained. The awful storm of God's wrath has spent itself. The darkness is ended. The sword of divine justice is done. The wages of sin have been paid. The prophecies of His sufferings are all fulfilled. The Cross has been "endured." Divine holiness has been fully satisfied (Isa 53:11). With a cry of triumph—a loud cry, a cry which reverberated throughout the entire universe—Jesus exclaims, "It is finished." The shame, the suffering and agony, are past. Never again shall He experience pain. Never again shall He endure the contradiction of sinners against Himself. Never again shall He be in the hands of Satan. Never again shall the light of God's countenance be hidden from Him. Blessed be God, all that is finished! "It is finished."

Jesus is concerned in the work of Redemption: He was the One who came here to die for sinners. He is the One who now gives spiritual illumination and understanding, and guides into the truth. Before the Lord Jesus came to this earth, a definite work was committed to Him. In the volume of the book it was written of Him, and He came to do the recorded will of God. Even as a boy of twelve the "Father's business" was before His heart and occupied His attention. Again, in John 5:36 we find Him saying, "But I have greater witness than that of John: for the works which the Father hath given me to finish, the same works that I do." And on the last night before His death, in that wonderful high priestly prayer, we find Him saying, "I have glorified thee on the earth: I have finished the work which thou gavest me to do" (John 17:4).

The mission upon which God had sent His Son into the world was now accomplished. It was not actually finished till He breathed His last, but death was only an instant ahead, and in anticipation of it He cries "It is finished." The demanding work is done. The divinely-given task is performed. A work more honorable and momentous than ever entrusted to man or angels, has been completed. That for which He had left heaven's glory that for which He had taken upon Him the form of a servant, that for which He had remained upon earth for thirty-three years to do, was now consummated. Nothing remained to be added. The goal of the Incarnation is reached. With what joyous triumph must He here have viewed the costly work which, committed to Him, had now been perfected!

"It is finished." The mission upon which God had sent His Son into the world was accomplished. That which had been eternally purposed had come to pass. The plan of God had been fully carried out.

Because He is the Most High, God's will, cannot be thwarted. Because He is supreme, God's counsel must stand. Because He is almighty, God's purpose cannot be overthrown.
"But he is in one mind, and who can turn him? And what his soul desireth, even that he doeth" (Job 23:13). "I know that thou canst do everything, and that no thought can be withholding from thee" (Job 42:2). "But our God is in the heavens: He hath done whatsoever he hath pleased" (Psa 115:3). "There is no wisdom nor understanding nor counsel against the Lord" (Pro 21:30). "For the Lord of hosts hath purposed, and who shall disannul it? And His hand is stretched out, and who shall turn it back?" (Isa 14:27). "Remember the former things of old: for I am God, and there is none else; I am God, and there is none like me: Declaring the end from the beginning, and from ancient times the things that are not yet done, saying, My counsel shall stand, and I will do all my pleasure" (Isa 46:9-10). "And all the inhabitants of the earth are reputed as nothing: and he doeth according to his will in the army of heaven, and among the inhabitants of the earth: and none can stay his hand, or say unto him, What doest thou?" (Dan 4:35). And, in the triumphant cry of the Jesus— "It is finished"—we have a prophecy and pledge of the ultimate carrying out of God's plan completely. At the end of time, when everything is wound up, and God's purpose has been fully consummated, when everything has been done which He before determined should be done, then shall it be said again, "It is finished."

"It is finished."
4. Here we see the accomplishment of the Atonement. Above we have spoken of Christ reaching the goal of the Incarnation, and of the consummation of His mission to the earth; what that goal and mission was, the Scriptures plainly reveal. The Son of Man came here "to seek and to save that which was lost" (Luke 19:10). Christ Jesus came into the world "to save sinners" (1Ti 1:15). God sent forth His Son, born of a woman, "to redeem them that were under the law" (Gal 4:5). He was manifested "to take away our sins" (1Jo 3:5). And all this involved the Cross. The "lost" which He came to seek could only be found there—in the place of death and under the condemnation of God. Sinners could be "saved" only by One taking their place and bearing their iniquities. They who were under the Law could be "redeemed" only by Another fulfilling its requirements and suffering its curse. Our sins could be "taken away" only by their being blotted out by the precious blood of Christ. The demands of justice must be met; the requirements of God's holiness must be satisfied; the awful debt we incurred must be paid. And on the Cross, this was done; done by none less than the Son of God; done perfectly; done once for all.

"It is finished."
That to which so many types looked forward, was now accomplished. A covering from sin and its shame, typified by the coats of skin with which the Lord God clothed our first parents, was now provided. The more excellent sacrifice, typified by Abel's lamb, had now been offered. A shelter from the storm of divine judgment, typified by the Ark of Noah, was now furnished. The only-begotten and well-beloved Son, typified by Abraham's offering up of Isaac, had already been placed upon the altar. A protection from the avenging angel, typified by the shed blood of the Passover-lamb, was now supplied. A cure from the serpent's bite, typified by the serpent of

brass upon the pole, was now made ready for sinners. The providing of a life-giving fountain, typified by Moses striking the rock, was now affected.

"It is finished." The Greek word here, teleo, is translated variously in the New Testament. A glance at some of the different renderings in other passages will enable us to discern the fullness and finality of the term used by Jesus. In Matthew 11:1, teleo is rendered as follows, "When Jesus had made an end of commanding his twelve disciples, he departed thence." In Matthew 17:24 it is rendered, "They that received tribute money came to Peter, and said, Doth not your master pay tribute?" In Luke 2:39, it is rendered, "And when they had performed all things according to the Law of the Lord, they returned into Galilee." In Luke 18:31, it is rendered, "All things that are written by the prophets concerning the Son shall be accomplished."

"It is finished." He cried: it is "made an end of"; it is "paid"; it is "performed"; it is "accomplished." What was made an end of? —our sins and their guilt. What was "paid?"—the price of our redemption. What was "performed?"—the utmost requirements of the Law. What was "accomplished?"—the work which the Father had given Him to do. What was "finished?"— the making of atonement. God has furnished at least four proofs that Christ did finish the work which was given Him to do. First, in the rending of the veil, which showed that the way to God was now open. Second, in the raising of Christ from the dead, which evidenced that God had accepted His sacrifice. Third, the exaltation of Christ to His own right hand, which demonstrated the value of Christ's work and the Father's delight in His person. Fourth, the sending to earth of the Holy Spirit to apply the virtues and benefits of Christ's atoning death.

"It is finished." What was "finished?"—the work of atonement. What is the value of that to us? This: to the sinner, it is a message of glad tidings. All that a Holy God requires has been done. Nothing is left for the sinner to add. No works from us are demanded as the price of our salvation. All that is necessary for the sinner is to rest now by faith upon what Christ did. "The gift of God is eternal life through Jesus Christ our Lord" (Rom 6:23). To the believer, the knowledge that the atoning work of Christ is finished brings a sweet relief over against all the defects and imperfections of his services. There is nothing "finished" that we do: all our duties are imperfect. There is much of sin and vanity in the very best of our efforts, but the grand relief is that we are "complete" in Christ (Col 2:10)! Christ and His finished work are the ground of all our hopes. "It is finished."

5. Here we see the end of our sins. The sins of the believer, all of them, were transferred to the Jesus. As the Scripture says, "The Lord hath laid on him the iniquities of us all" (Isa 53:6). If then God laid my iniquities on Christ, they are no longer on me. Sin there is in me, for the old Adamic nature remains in the believer till death or till Christ's return, should He come before I die; but there is no sin on me. This distinction between sin in and sin on, is a vital one, and there should be little difficulty in apprehending it. If I were to say the judge passed sentence on a criminal, and that he is now under sentence of death, everyone would understand what I meant. In like manner, everyone out of Christ has the sentence of God's condemnation resting upon him. But when a sinner believes in the Lord Jesus, and receives Him as his Lord and Master, obey the salvation message according to (Acts 2:38-39) he is no longer "under condemnation"— sin is no longer on him, that is, the guilt, the condemnation, the penalty of sin, is no longer upon him. And why? Because Christ bore our sins in His own body on the tree (1Pe 2:24)—the guilt,

condemnation, and penalty of our sins, was transferred to our substitute. Hence, because my sins were transferred to Christ, they are no more upon me.

This precious truth was strikingly illustrated in Old Testament times regarding Israel's annual Day of Atonement. On that day, Aaron, the high priest (a type of Christ), made satisfaction to God for the sins which Israel had committed during the previous year. The way this was done is described in Leviticus 16. Two goats were taken and presented before the Lord at the door of the tabernacle: this was before anything was done with them: it represented Christ being sent and presenting Himself, offering to come into this world and be the Savior of sinners. One of the goats was then taken and killed, and its blood was carried into the tabernacle, within the veil, into the Holy of Holies, and there it was sprinkled before and upon the mercy seat—foreshadowing Christ offering Himself as a sacrifice, to meet the demands of His justice and satisfy the requirements of His holiness.

Then we read that Aaron came out of the tabernacle and laid both his hands upon the head of the second (living) goat— signifying an act of identification by which Aaron is the representative of the whole nation, identified the people with it, acknowledging that its doom was what their sins merited, and which, today, corresponds with the hands of faith laying hold of Christ and identifying ourselves with Him in His Death. Having laid his hands on the head of the live goat, Aaron now confessed over him "all the iniquities of the children of Israel, and all their transgressions in all their sins, putting them upon the head of the goat" (Lev 16:21). Thus, were Israel's sins transferred to their substitute. Finally, we are told, "And the goat shall bear upon him all their iniquities unto a land not inhabited: and he shall let go the goat in the wilderness" (Lev 16:22). The goat bearing Israel's sins, was taken unto an uninhabited wilderness, and the people of God saw him and their sins no more! In type this was Christ taking our sins into that desolate land where God was not and there making an end of them. The Cross of Christ then is the grave of our sins!

"It is finished."
6. Here we see the fulfillment of the Law's requirements. "The law is holy, and the commandment holy, and just and good" (Rom 7:12). How could it be anything less when Jehovah Himself had framed and given it! The fault lay not in the Law but in man who, being depraved and sinful, could not keep it. Yet that Law must be kept, and kept by a man, so that the Law might be honored and magnified, and its giver vindicated. Therefore, we read, "For what the law could not do, in that it was weak through the flesh, God sending his own Son, in the likeness of sinful flesh, and for sin, condemned sin in the flesh: that the righteousness of the law might be fulfilled in [not by] us, who walk not after flesh, but after the Spirit" (Rom 8:3-4). The "weakness" here is that of fallen man. The sending forth of God's Son in the likeness of sin's flesh (Greek) refers to the Incarnation: as we read in another Scripture, "God sent forth his Son, born of a woman, born under the law, that he might redeem them that were under the law" (Gal 4:4-5 RV). Yes, the Jesus was born "under the law," born under it that He might keep it perfectly in thought, word, and deed. "Think not that I am come to destroy the law, or the prophets: I am not come to destroy, but to fulfill" (Mat 5:17); such was His claim.

But not only did Jesus keep the precepts of the Law, He also suffered its penalty and endured its curse. We had broken it, and taking our place, He must receive its just sentence. Having received its penalty and endured its curse, the demands of the Law are fully met, and justice is satisfied. Therefore, is it written of believers, "Christ hath redeemed us from the curse of the law, being made a curse for us" (Gal 3:13). And again, "For Christ is the end of the law for righteousness to everyone that believeth" (Rom 10:4). And yet again, "For ye are not under the law, but under grace" (Rom 6:14). "It is finished." "Free from the Law, Jesus hath bled, and there is remission, cursed by the law and bruised by the fall, Grace hath redeemed us once for all."

7. Here we see the destruction of Satan's power. See it by faith. The Cross sounded the death of the devil's power. To human appearances it looked like the moment of his greatest triumph, yet, it was the hour of his ultimate defeat. In view of the Cross Jesus declared, "Now is the judgment of this world: now shall the prince of this world be cast out" (Joh 12:31). It is true that Satan has not yet been chained and cast into the bottomless pit, nevertheless, sentence has been passed (though not yet executed); his doom is certain; and his power is already broken so far as believers are concerned.

For the Christian, the devil is a vanquished foe. He was defeated by Christ at the Cross— "that through death he might destroy him that had the power of death, that is, the devil" (Hebrew 2:14). Believers have already been "delivered from the power of darkness" and translated into the kingdom of God's dear Son (Col 1:13). Satan, then, should be treated as a defeated enemy. No longer has he any legitimate claim upon us. Once we were his lawful "captives"; but now God worketh in us both to will and to do of His good pleasure. All that we now must do is to "resist the devil," and the promise is, "he will flee from you" (James 4:7).

"It is finished." Here was the triumphant answer to the rage of man and the enmity of Satan. It tells of the perfect work which meets sin in the place of judgment. All was completed just as God would have it, just as the prophets had foretold, just as the Old Testament ceremonial had foreshadowed, just as divine holiness demanded, and just as sinners needed. How strikingly appropriate is this sixth Cross-utterance of Jesus found in John's Gospel—the Gospel which displays the glory of Christ's deity! He seals it with His own words, attesting it is complete, and giving it the all-sufficient sanction of His own approval. Jesus says, "It is finished"—who then dare doubt or question it.

"It is finished." Reader, do you believe it? or, are you trying to add something of your own to the finished work of Christ to secure the favor of God? All you must do is to accept the pardon which He purchased. God is satisfied with His work on the cross, why are not you? Sinner, the moment you believe Jesus' testimony that it is finished, that moment every sin you have committed is blotted out, and you stand accepted in Christ! O would you not like to possess the assurance that there is nothing between your soul and God? Would you not like to know that every sin had been atoned for and put away? Then believe what God's Word says about Christ's death. Rest not on your feelings and experiences but on the written Word. There is only one way of finding peace, deliverance, wholeness, salvation, victory over the "it" and that is through faith in the shed blood of Jesus the of Lamb God. It is time to "Get Rid of "it", Before "it" Gets Rid of You".

"It is finished." Do you really believe it? Or, are you endeavoring to add something of your own to it and thus merit the favor of God? By continuing to hold on and struggle, seeking other sources to deal with the "it" in your life, you are nullifying the finished work of Christ by your own miserable additions to it!". The Gospel of God's grace, and the finished work of Christ is sufficient for our souls to rest upon. In the pages of this book, God uses forceful object lessons and His Word to show you, "How to Get Rid of "it", before "it" Gets Rid of You". It is a grave mistake not to embrace the Word of God, and cast yourself by faith upon what Christ had done for you.

Victory was given to us by way of the cross. Whatever your "it" or "its" might be, "it" has come to kill, steal and destroy you. Make a conscious effort to explore this information given in this book and expose the enemy of your soul. Let's "Get Rid of "it". After all, "It is Finished"

CHAPTER ONE

What is "it"?

We are all created with a basic need to be loved. God created us to both give and receive love, but though damaged emotions, our capacity to receive love can be dramatically hindered. Ignorance of God's love will also hinder us from receiving the great and glorious love that He has for us. **The root of most "its" is a lack of love being received by that person.** Many of us have been damaged emotionally by rejection, abandonment, abuse, etc., and thereby our capacity to receive love has been reduced. **Only an emotionally healthy person is capable of both giving and receiving love as God intended.**

Self-worth issues can hinder love

Self-worth issues are rooted in believing that we are not worthy or deserve to be loved. When we believe that we are unlovable, we will unconsciously reject any love that comes our way. We won't believe the love, because we believe in our hearts that we are not worthy. **Self-worth issues are all rooted in our failing to see who we really are in Christ.**

If you walked into a gallery of world-class art, and pointed to a painting, saying, "That is the ugliest thing I've ever seen! Who painted that??" Now let's say the artist was standing right next to you. How do you think that would make him feel? Do you realize we are the artwork of God, a special painting crafted together by the master painter? Do you think it brings Him honor when we look down on ourselves? **We need to stop putting down what God has made.**

Many times, we have self-unforgiveness issues because we blame ourselves for something, or we've done something we deeply regret, and we simply cannot let it go. We need to realize that Jesus has forgiven us of all our failures, and we need to start seeing ourselves as forgiven. Otherwise, we're denying the work of Christ in our life! **If God forgave you, and you're still beating yourself up, then you don't really believe what Jesus did for you.** It's that simple!

Just as we must forgive others (see Matthew 18:21-35), we need to forgive ourselves just the same. Self-hate has been known to be the root behind diseases such as lupus and Crohn's disease, as well as other auto-immune diseases. We need to stop holding ourselves accountable for that which Jesus has set us free from.

If we want to be in faith, we need to BELIEVE what Jesus did for us, and part of that believing is seeing ourselves as forgiven and clothed with the righteousness of God, which is upon all who believe in the finished work of Christ. Without faith, it is

16

impossible to please God (see Hebrews 11:6), so if you want to please God, start taking the finished work of the cross seriously, and begin to see yourself as forgiven, washed clean, and clothed in the righteousness of God. For the righteousness (right standing with God) is upon all who believe:

> *"Even the righteousness of God which is by faith of Jesus Christ unto all and upon all them that believe..." (Romans 3:22 KJV)*

Unforgiveness is rooted in a lack of realization of how much God has forgiven us, and therefore we're not thankful for the steep and terrible price that Jesus paid for our own failures. Therefore, it is so important to mediate on what Jesus did for us, until it transforms our heart. The message of Jesus' work for us is what causes faith to arise in our hearts and transforms us from the inside out (read Romans 10:8-17).

Learning to see yourself as God sees you, and forgive yourself because you want to please God and be in faith and be thankful for what Jesus did for you, is the biggest step in overcoming self-worth issues. Of course, there are spirits that may need to be driven out as well, such as self-hate, guilt, condemnation, etc.

Receiving the love God has for us

When it comes to God's love for us, that's obvious, considering how He loves even the sinner so much that Jesus came to die for them. Anybody who knows the message of the cross, has some knowledge of God's love for us. However, many times, we blame God for our problems, and so we don't believe the love that He has for us. Not only do we blame Him for our problems, many times we think that God gave us the sickness or problem in our life to teach us something. Nothing could be further from the truth! Jesus tells us clearly who came to kill, steal, and destroy, and who came so that we could have life and have it in abundance.

> *"The thief cometh not, but for to steal, and to kill, and to destroy: I am come that they might have life, and that they might have it more abundantly." (John 10:10 KJV)*

If we are going to receive the love that God has for us, we need to get our thinking straightened out. He's not the one behind our problems, but rather Jesus paid the full price so that we can be forgiven all our sins, both physically and emotionally healed, and blessed.

> *"When the even was come, they brought unto him many that were possessed with devils: and he cast out the spirits with his word, and healed all that were sick: That it might be fulfilled which was spoken by Esaias the prophet, saying, Himself took our infirmities, and bare our sicknesses." (Matthew 8:16-17 KJV)*

Look at how good God's heart is toward mankind! Not only did Jesus heal them, but He proved the blessings of the covenant we have with Him today concerning our healing and deliverance. Isn't He good toward us? **The reason why things happen to us, is because we live in a fallen world that is under the control of the evil one.** It's not God's fault. He loves you. Jesus died for you.

Settling the fact that God loves you and is good toward you is crucial to restoring your God-given capacity to receive His love. If you can't receive His love, then you need to stop and ask yourself four questions:

1. Am I blaming God for anything bad that happened to me?

2. Have I been emotionally wounded in such a way that it is hindering my ability to freely receive love as God intended me to?

3. Do I have knowledge and revelation of how much God loves me? Do I have a solid Biblical understanding of how I am loved with the same kind of love that the Father has for Jesus?

4. Is there a self-worth issue that makes me feel unworthy to be loved?

Settling these issues lays a foundation for breaking free from the power of the "IT". You must repair the damage and faulty thinking which hinders your ability to receive the love that God has for you.

How do you know if you are receiving God's love or if it's hindered? **If you are not passionate about Jesus, then somewhere your ability to receive His love is hindered.**

If you are living a life without receiving God's love in your heart daily, you are missing out on the most fulfilling life you can have here on this earth. To know God's love, which surpasses all understanding (see Philippians 4:7), dispels all our fears and gives us a sense of peace and joy that we could never otherwise know.

> *"And we have known and believed the love that God hath to us. God is love; and he that dwelleth in love dwelleth in God, and God in him. Herein is our love made perfect, that we may have boldness in the day of judgment: because as he is, so are we in this world. There is no fear in love; but perfect love casteth out fear: because fear hath torment. He that feareth is not made perfect in love." (1 John 4:16-18 KJV)*

What exactly is "it"?

An "it" is formed when we try to use something other than God, to meet our need to be loved. When our ability to receive God's love into our hearts is hindered, we will feel like something is missing, and seek to fill that void with something else. When that thing, whatever it might be, fills that void, we grow to love "it" because it's meeting a need. Over time, we establish a relationship with that thing, and when it comes time to depart, it's like breaking up a relationship. That's why the "it" is so destructive; we've relied on that thing to meet a need and we've established a relationship with it. Now when it's time to break up the love, it isn't so easy to say goodbye.

One widespread problem that we see when we try to deal with "it", is where we give up one "it" successfully, only to find yourself with another "it". We might quit drinking only to start overeating, for example. We might think we're finding victory, but all we're really doing is trading one "it" for another "it". This is because something must fill the love-void in our hearts, and if it's not one thing, it will be another.

What about cutting or self-harm?

Cutting or self-mutation is a special type of "it", where there's a need to either release pain in a person's heart or the person believes that they deserve to be punished for their failures. In these cases, the person certainly has an issue receiving the love that God has for them but there's another type of root that needs to be addressed as well. There's emotional pain or guilt that the person is dealing with that needs to be resolved. Finding out what happened and receiving Christ's truth concerning those areas is important for their healing. Any bondage involving guilt will need to be resolved through realizing and accepting the work of Christ on the cross for that person and they will likely need spirits of guilt, condemnation, self-hate, etc. driven out in Jesus' name. Again, getting the person to see them self for who they really are in Christ, forgiven, loved, and blessed, is crucial to lasting freedom from self-hate issues.

See yourself as lovable!

The key in uprooting most "its" is to deal with the underlying issues which are limiting their capacity to freely receive love from God and others, along with dealing with any self-worth issues by establishing an understanding of your true identity in Christ. **Coming to a place where you believe you are lovable is key to receiving love in general**, so dealing with self-worth issues is an important key to breaking down the walls which keep us from feeling loved. The only way to obtain a true sense of worth and value is to get a revelation of how much you are loved by God, who sent His son Jesus to die for you.

Discovering the root

To discover the root of your "it", you need to get real honest with yourself. Many times, we are in denial about the pain we are feeling. Figuring out what is the root of a bondage is all about asking the right questions, and that is especially important when it comes to uprooting an "it". Why don't we feel loved? Do we feel unlovable? (Let's stop right there; if we feel unlovable, then you've just discovered a self-worth issue that will need to be addressed.) Are you passionate about Jesus? If not, then something in hindering you from realizing how much you are loved by Him who died for you. Do you see yourself as forgiven and loved by the God because of what He did for you?

As you discover emotional wounds, you'll need to forgive (others, yourself, and God) and invite Jesus to come and heal the damage in your heart. If you don't realize how much God loves you, then you'll need to spend some time learning about what Jesus did for you on the cross, and what a terrible price He paid because He loved you so very much. Often breaking out of an "it" is a combination of emotional healing, learning about who you are in Christ, forgiving (yourself, others, and God), overcoming self-worth issues by changing how you see yourself (in light of how God sees and loves you), and casting out any spirits that came in and are enforcing the destructive behavior. Spirits behind guilt, condemnation, etc. also need to be driven out, as they seek to keep us from fully seeing what Jesus did for us on the cross.

Dealing with the issues underlying an "it" is key to uprooting it permanently. If you want lasting freedom and wholeness in this area of your life, you will have to deal with the issues that have limited your capacity to receive love, especially the love that God has for you.

CHAPTER TWO

The "it" of Spiritual Warfare

DEFINITION: Spiritual warfare refers to the battles waged by believers against our spiritual enemies--Satan, demons, and the spiritual forces of evil.

FACTS ABOUT SPIRITUAL WARFARE:

There are two spiritual kingdoms. The Kingdom of Satan and the Kingdom of God (Luke 4:5-6). The Kingdom of Satan consists of Satan himself, spiritual beings called demons, and all people who live in sin and rebellion against God. God's Kingdom consists of God (the Father, Son, and Holy Spirit, all are one), angels, and all people who live in loving submission to Him.

Every person alive is a resident of one of these two kingdoms, the Kingdom of Satan or the Kingdom of God. There is no neutral ground (Matthew 12:30). You become a resident of God's Kingdom by being born again and becoming a believer in Jesus Christ (John 3:16). (Acts 2:38-39)

Spiritual warfare began when Lucifer, who was originally a beautiful angel of prominence, rebelled against God (Isaiah 14:12-17; Ezekiel 28:12-19; Revelation 12:7-8).

The spiritual battle was manifested on earth when Adam and Eve yielded to Satan in the Garden of Eden (Genesis 3).

All the battles that you face in life, whether spiritual, emotional, mental, financial, or relational are outward manifestations of a direct or indirect spiritual cause. Although in the natural world things often appear to be simply "circumstances" of life, the basis of these natural events originate in the spiritual world. Spiritual warfare is a spiritual battle which is manifested in the natural world.

Spiritual warfare is not against flesh and blood. The battle is against the evil forces that would hinder your walk with God, the Word of God manifested in your life, your worship of God, and your work for Him.

DEALING WITH SPIRITUAL WARFARE:

Prepare for effective spiritual battle by arming yourself with spiritual weapons. These include:

      -The belt of truth by gaining knowledge and understanding (Ephesians 6:14).
      -The breastplate of righteousness--spiritual protection that comes by living the way the Word mandates (Ephesians 6:14).
      -Spiritual shoes--protection that comes from the gospel of Jesus Christ (Ephesians 6:15).
      -The shield of faith which stops the fiery darts from the enemy (Ephesians 6:16).
      -The helmet of salvation, which protects your mind, soul, and spirit (Ephesians 6:17).

21

-The sword of the Spirit, which is the Word of God (Ephesians 6:17).
-Prayer (Ephesians 6:18).
-The blood of Jesus (Revelation 12:11).
-Your testimony (Revelation 12:11).
-The name of Jesus (Mark 16:17).
-Praise and worship (Psalm 59:16-17).
-Fasting (the books of Esther and Jonah).

Use these biblical strategies to win spiritual battles.

Submit and resist. If you submit yourself to God and resist the devil, he will flee from you (James 4:7). To resist means to "stand firm against and oppose the enemy at every point."

Do not give place to the devil. Do not leave room for Satan to operate (Ephesians 4:27). Giving "place" to the devil is providing him a foothold from where he can operate in your life-- for examples through alcohol, drugs, pornography, immorality, witchcraft, cults, rebellion, etc.

Recover yourself from the devil. You have a responsibility to recover yourself from Satan's snare. You must cooperate with God for deliverance (2 Timothy 2:26).

Abstain from fleshly lusts. To "abstain" means "to deliberately refrain evil practices. The lusts of the flesh are listed in Galatians 5:19-21 as conduct from which you must abstain. Fleshly lusts war against your spirit (1 Peter 2:11).

Try the spirits. Be alert for the deceptions of the enemy (2 Peter 3: 17; 1 Timothy 4:1).

Reject false teachers. A false teacher is one who teaches incorrect doctrines and fails to live up to the mandates of God's Word (2 John 10-11).

Lay aside worldly entanglements. To be a good solider for Jesus, you must lay aside worldly affairs (2 Timothy 2:4).

Arm yourself with the mind of Christ. The mind of Jesus is not automatically developed in you. You must "let" or "permit" it to be developed (1 Peter 4: 1; Philippians 2:5-8; Romans 12:1-2).

Pull and cast down strongholds. One of the goals of offensive warfare is to pull and cast down the strongholds of the enemy (2 Corinthians 10:4-5). To "pull down" means "to take down by effort or force." To "cast" means "to throw or hurl." You are told to cast off the works of darkness (Romans 13: 12) and cast out demon powers (Matthew 10:8). You are to demolish arguments and pretensions and to take captive any thought that is contrary to the thoughts of Christ.

Bind and loose. You have the power to bind the forces of evil and loose the forces of good (Matthew 16:19). For example, you can bind the spirit of iniquity at work in the life of a lost loved one and release the spirit of adoption (a ministry of the Holy Spirit) to work in that person's life.

WHAT GOD'S WORD SAYS ABOUT SPIRITUAL WARFARE:

But I will sing of your strength, in the morning I will sing of your love; for you are my fortress, my refuge in times of trouble. (Psalm 59:16)

How you have fallen from heaven, O morning star, son of the dawn! You have been cast down to the earth, you who once laid low the nations! You said in your heart, "I will ascend to heaven; I will raise my throne above the stars of God; I will sit enthroned on the mount of assembly, on the utmost heights of the sacred mountain.   I will ascend above the tops of the clouds; I will make myself like the Most High." But you are brought down to the grave, to the depths of the pit. (Isaiah 14:12-15)

See also Ezekiel 28:12-19.

"He who is not with me is against me..." (Matthew 12:30)

I will give you the keys of the kingdom of heaven; whatever you bind on earth will be bound in heaven, and whatever you loose on earth will be loosed in heaven. (Matthew 16:19)

And these signs will accompany those who believe: In my Name, they will drive out demons; they will speak in new tongues; they will pick up snakes with their hands; and when they drink deadly poison, it will not hurt them at all; they will place their hands on sick people, and they will get well.   (Mark 16:17-18)

Read about the temptation of Jesus in Luke 4:1-13. Note that strategies used by Satan and how Jesus met each one with the Word of God.

He replied, "I saw Satan fall like lightning from heaven. I have given you authority to trample on snakes and scorpions and to overcome all the power of the enemy; nothing will harm you." (Luke 10:18-19)

The thief comes only to steal and kill and destroy; I have come that they may have life, and have it to the full. (John 10:10)

I beseech you therefore, brethren, by the mercies of God, that you present your bodies a living sacrifice, holy, acceptable to God, which is your reasonable service. And do not be conformed to this world, but be transformed by the renewing of your mind, that you may prove what is that good and acceptable and perfect will of God. (Romans 12:1-2, NKJV)

...Lest Satan should get an advantage of us: for we are not ignorant of his devices. (2 Corinthians 2:11)

The weapons we fight with are not the weapons of the world. On the contrary, they have divine power to demolish strongholds. We demolish arguments and every pretension that sets itself up against the knowledge of God, and we take captive every thought to make it obedient to Christ. (2 Corinthians 10:4-5)

Finally, be strong in the Lord and in his mighty power. Put on the full armor of God so that you can take your stand against the devil's schemes. For our struggle is not against flesh and blood, but against the rulers, against the authorities, against the powers of this dark world and against the spiritual forces of evil in the heavenly realms. Therefore, put on the full armor of God, so that when the day of evil comes, you may be able to stand your ground, and after you have done everything, to stand. Stand firm then, with the belt of truth buckled around your waist, with the breastplate of righteousness in place, and with your feet fitted with the readiness that comes from the gospel of peace. In addition to all this, take up the shield of faith, with which you can extinguish all the flaming arrows of the evil one. Take the helmet of salvation and the sword of the Spirit, which is the word of God. And pray in the Spirit on all occasions with all kinds of prayers and requests. With this in mind, be alert and always keep on praying for all the saints. (Ephesians 6:10-18)

Fight the good fight of the faith. Take hold of the eternal life to which you were called when you made your good confession in the presence of many witnesses. (1 Timothy 6:12)

For God did not give us a spirit of timidity, but a spirit of power, of love and of self-discipline. (2 Timothy 1:7)

...and that they will come to their senses and escape from the trap of the devil, who has taken them captive to do his will. (2 Timothy 2:26)

For the word of God is living and active. Sharper than any double-edged sword, it penetrates even to dividing soul and spirit, joints and marrow; it judges the thoughts and attitudes of the heart. (Hebrews 4:12)

Submit yourselves, then, to God. Resist the devil, and he will flee from you. (James 4:7)

Therefore, since Christ suffered in his body, arm yourselves also with the same attitude... (1 Peter 4:1)

Be self-controlled and alert. Your enemy the devil prowls around like a roaring lion looking for someone to devour. Resist him, standing firm in the faith, because you know that your brothers throughout the world are undergoing the same kind of sufferings. (1 Peter 5:8-9)

He who does what is sinful is of the devil, because the devil has been sinning from the beginning. The reason the Son of God appeared was to destroy the devil's work. (1 John 3:8)

If anyone comes to you and does not bring this teaching, do not take him into your house or welcome him. (2 John 1:11)

And there was war in heaven. Michael and his angels fought against the dragon, and the dragon and his angels fought back. But he was not strong enough, and they lost their place in heaven. The great dragon was hurled down--that ancient serpent called the devil, or Satan, who leads the whole world astray. He was hurled to the earth, and his angels with him. (Revelation 12:7-9)

They overcame him by the blood of the Lamb and by the word of their testimony; they did not love their lives so much as to shrink from death. (Revelation 12:11)

Read the story of Elisha in 2 Kings 6:8-22 for further insights into spiritual warfare.

CHAPTER THREE

The "it" of Denying the Lord

DEFINITION: To deny someone or something is to be ashamed of them, fail to acknowledge them, or claim they do not exist. Biblically, denying the Lord is a failure to acknowledge Him and the truth of His Word. People who deny the existence of God are called atheists.

FACTS ABOUT DENYING THE LORD:

If you deny the existence of God, you are a fool. *"The fool says in his heart, 'There is no God'* "(Psalm 14:1).

Denying the Lord includes denying there is a God; denying the deity of Jesus Christ; denying the inspiration of God's Word; denying the work of God; denying the saving work of Christ; denying your faith; and denial by your sinful actions.

What you say and do are both important. If you confess Christ and then live like a sinner, you are denying God's work in your life.

Denying the Lord is not the unpardonable sin.   It can be forgiven through confession and repentance.   If you do not repent, however, God also will deny you (Matthew 10:32-33).

DEALING WITH DENYING THE LORD:

Confess your sin to God and ask forgiveness. Denying the Lord is sin, and as in the case of all sin, you must confess and repent of it.

Make a positive confession based on the Word. Confess the existence of God, your belief in Him and His Word, and in the atoning work of Jesus Christ.

Confess the Lord before others. If you have previously denied God, His Word, or His work in your life before certain people or groups, make it a point to go back and confess the Lord in front of these people.

WHAT GOD'S WORD SAYS ABOUT DENYING THE LORD:

The fool says in his heart, "There is no God." (Psalm 14:1)

I speak of your faithfulness and salvation. I do not conceal your love and your truth from the great assembly. (Psalm 40:10)

Whoever acknowledges me before men, I will also acknowledge him before my Father in heaven. But whoever disowns me before men, I will disown him before my Father in heaven. (Matthew 10:32-33)

If anyone is ashamed of me and my words in this adulterous and sinful generation, the Son of Man will be ashamed of him when he comes in his Father's glory with the holy angels. (Mark 8:38)

He who listens to you listens to me; he who rejects you rejects me; but he who rejects me rejects him who sent me. (Luke 10:16)

He who is not with me is against me, and he who does not gather with me, scatters. (Luke 11:23)

And anyone who does not carry his cross and follow me cannot be my disciple. (Luke 14:27)

There is a judge for the one who rejects me and does not accept my words; that very word which I spoke will condemn him at the last day. (John 12:48)

I am not ashamed of the gospel, because it is the power of God for the salvation of everyone who believes: first for the Jew, then for the Gentile. (Romans 1:16)

Pray also for me, that whenever I open my mouth, words may be given me so that I will fearlessly make known the mystery of the gospel, for which I am ambassador in chains. Pray that I may declare it fearlessly, as I should. (Ephesians 6:19-20)

I eagerly expect and hope that I will in no way be ashamed, but will have sufficient courage so that now as always Christ will be exalted in my body, whether by life or by death. (Philippians 1:20)

Through Jesus, therefore, let us continually offer to God sacrifice of praise--the fruit of lips that confess his name. (Hebrews 13:15)

But there were also false prophets among the people, just as there will be false teachers among you. They will secretly introduce destructive heresies, even denying the sovereign Lord who bought them--bringing swift destruction on themselves. Many will follow their shameful ways and will bring the way of truth into disrepute. (2 Peter 2:1-2)

No one who denies the Son has the Father; whoever acknowledges the Son has the Father also. (1 John 2:23)

If anyone acknowledges that Jesus is the Son of God, God lives in him and he in God. (1 John 4:15)

CHAPTER FOUR

The "it" of Cults and False Doctrines

DEFINITION: A cult is any group whose beliefs differ from the basic tenets of God's Word and whose members do not acknowledge Jesus Christ as the Son of God. False doctrine is any teaching or belief that cannot be documented by the written Word of God.

FACTS ABOUT CULTS AND FALSE DOCTRINES:

There are many false religions and cults. You must follow the truth of God's Word, not the so-called revelations of man.

Cults often emerge from claims of personal revelation. Such revelations, if not in harmony with the Word of God, should be rejected (Galatians 1:8-9).

Cults often incorporate partial truths in their doctrines. For example, they may talk about the love of God and love for one another, yet deny the reality of the sacrifice of Jesus Christ for sin.

Cults always present other ways to God. There are "many ways to God", they claim. But the Bible says*: "It is by the name of Jesus Christ of Nazareth, whom you crucified but whom God raised from the dead, that this man stands before you healed. He is "the stone you builders rejected, which has become the capstone.' Salvation is found in no one else, for there is no other name under heaven given to men by which we must be saved." (Acts 4:10-12)*

Common characteristics of cults and false doctrines include:
   -Dictatorial Leadership: Cults cluster around domineering personalities who have
      absolute authority and are accountable to no one.
   -Exclusive: Cults adopt the attitude that they are the only group with divine truth.
   They exclude from fellowship others who disagree with them.
   -Legalistic: Cults usually have strict rules of belief and behavior which have no
      Scriptural basis.
   -Defensive: Cult members are usually led to believe that society, organized religion,
      and/or governments are against them.
   -Oppressive: Cult members are usually manipulated, controlled, and oppressed by the
      leadership.
   -Secretive: Many things about the cult are kept secret from outsiders.
   -Higher Revelation: Cults often claim "higher revelation" from God, a source of authority
      beyond the Scriptures
   -Anti-church: Cults vigorously oppose organized churches and their pastors.
   -Anti-family: Cults sometimes want their members to break ties with family who are not
      members.
   -Salvation by works. They emphasize what you do rather than the fact that all has
      been done by Christ to secure your salvation.

DEALING WITH CULTS AND FALSE DOCTRINES:

Ask God to forgive you if you have been involved with a cult or false doctrine.

Renounce any involvement with cults and false doctrines. Leave the cult. Leave the fellowship of those teaching false doctrines. Break all ties!

Pray for deliverance from the demonic influences involved in cults. Cults are doctrines perpetrated by devils (1 Timothy 4:1).

Reaffirm your commitment to God. Reaffirm your belief in God and that Jesus is the only way to God and His Word as the authoritative source of truth.

Renew your mind in the Word of God. Cults tend to "brainwash" their members, so you need to renew your mind in order to understand and receive the truth: *"Therefore, I urge you, brothers, in view of God's mercy, to offer your bodies as living sacrifices, holy and pleasing to God--this is your spiritual act of worship. Do not conform any longer to the pattern of this world, but be transformed by the renewing of your mind. Then you will be able to test and approve what God's will is--his good, pleasing and perfect will" (Romans 12:1-2).* Study God's Word--not books written by man. Compare everything you read, hear, or are taught to what the Word of God teaches.

Join a Bible-believing church. The church is the pillar and foundation of truth and will help you grow in the Lord (1 Timothy 3:15).

WHAT GOD'S WORD SAYS ABOUT CULTS AND FALSE DOCTRINES:

I gain understanding from your precepts; therefore, I hate every wrong path. (Psalm 119:104)

There is a way that seems right to a man, but its end is the way of death. (Proverbs 16:25)

For false Christs and false prophets will appear and perform great signs and miracles to deceive even the elect--if that were possible. See, I have told you ahead of time. (Matthew 24:24-25)

It is by the name of Jesus Christ of Nazareth, whom you crucified but whom God raised from the dead, that this man stands before you healed. He is 'the stone you builders rejected, which has become the capstone. Salvation is found in no one else, for there is no other name under heaven given to men by which we must be saved. (Acts 4:10-12)

Therefore, I urge you, brothers, in view of God's mercy, to offer your bodies as living sacrifices, holy and pleasing to God--this is your spiritual act of worship. Do not conform any longer to the pattern of this world, but be transformed by the renewing of your mind. Then you will be able to test and approve what God's will is--his good, pleasing and perfect will. (Romans 12:1-2)

For such are false apostles, deceitful workers, transforming themselves into the apostles of Christ. And no marvel; for Satan himself is transformed into an angel of light. (2 Corinthians 11: 13-14)

But even if we or an angel from heaven should preach a gospel other than the one we preached to you, let him be eternally condemned! As we have already said, so now I say again: If anybody is preaching to you a gospel other than what you accepted, let him be eternally condemned! (Galatians 1:8-9)

See to it that no one takes you captive through hollow and deceptive philosophy, which depends on human tradition and the basic principles of this world rather than on Christ. (Colossians 2:8)

Do your best to present yourself to God as one approved, a workman who does not need to be ashamed and who correctly handles the word of truth. Avoid godless chatter, because those who indulge in it will become more and more ungodly. Their teaching will spread like gangrene. (2 Timothy 2:15-17)

But evil men and impostors will grow worse and worse, deceiving and being deceived. But you must continue in the things which you have learned and been assured of, knowing from whom you have learned them, and that from childhood you have known the Holy Scriptures, which are able to make you wise for salvation through faith which is in Christ Jesus. (2 Timothy 3:13-15, NKJV)

For the time will come when they will not endure sound doctrine, but according to their own desires, because they have itching ears, they will heap up for themselves teachers; and they will turn their ears away from the truth, and be turned aside to fables. (2 Timothy 4:3-4)

Above all, you must understand that no prophecy of Scripture came about by the prophet's own interpretation. For prophecy never had its origin in the will of man, but men spoke from God as they were carried along by the Holy Spirit. (2 Peter 1:20-21)

But there were false prophets also among the people, even as there shall be false teachers among you, who privity shall bring in damnable heresies, even denying the Lord that bought them, and bring upon themselves swift destruction. And many shall follow their pernicious ways; by reason of whom the way of truth shall be evil spoken of. (2 Peter 2:1-2)

Who is the liar? It is the man who denies that Jesus is the Christ. Such a man is the antichrist--he denies the Father and the Son. No one who denies the Son has the Father; whoever acknowledges the Son has the Father also. (1 John 2:22-23)

Dear friends, do not believe every spirit, but test the spirits to see whether they are from God, because many false prophets have gone out into the world. This is how you can recognize the Spirit of God: Every spirit that acknowledges that Jesus Christ has come in the flesh is from God, but every spirit that does not acknowledge Jesus is not from God. This is the spirit of the antichrist, which you have heard is coming and even now is already in the world. (1 John 4:1-3)

Whoever transgresses and does not abide in the doctrine of Christ does not have God. He who abides in the doctrine of Christ has both the Father and the Son. If anyone comes to you and does not bring this doctrine, do not receive him into your house nor greet him; for he who greets him shares in his evil deeds. (2 John 9-11)

But you, beloved, remember the words which were spoken before by the apostles of our Lord Jesus Christ: how they told you that there would be mockers in the last time who would walk according to their own ungodly lusts. These are sensual persons, who cause divisions, not having the Spirit. But you, beloved, building yourselves up on your most holy faith, praying in the Holy Spirit, keep yourselves in the love of God, looking for the mercy of our Lord Jesus Christ unto eternal life. (Jude 17-21)

CHAPTER FIVE

The "it" of Blasphemy

DEFINITION: Blasphemy is disrespect shown towards God, His Word, or something that is deemed holy.

FACTS ABOUT BLASPHEMY:

Blasphemy can occur in various ways. You can blaspheme not only by what you say, but also by your conduct. Riotous, sinful behavior does not show respect towards God and His Word and is a form of blasphemy. Using God's name in vain as a curse word is blasphemy.

Blasphemy starts in the heart. Jesus said that blasphemy--as other sins--begins in the heart (Mark 7:20-23).

Blasphemy is sin. Jesus said one who blasphemed needs forgiveness (Mark 3:18).

DEALING WITH BLASPHEMY:

Identify your blasphemous behavior. Are you committing blasphemy by what you say or do?

Repent. Blasphemy is sin (Mark 7:20-23). As in all sinful behavior, it requires repentance.

Ask God to create a new heart in you. Since blasphemy comes from the heart, your heart needs to be changed. Claim this scripture: *"I will give you a new heart and put a new spirit in you; I will remove from you your heart of stone and give you a heart of flesh. And I will put my Spirit in you and move you to follow my decrees and be careful to keep my laws"* *(Ezekiel 36:26-27).*

WHAT GOD'S WORD SAYS ABOUT BLASPHEMY:

I tell you the truth, all the sins and blasphemies of men will be forgiven them. (Mark 3:28)

And He said, "What comes out of a man, that defiles a man. For from within, out of the heart of men, proceed evil thoughts, adulteries, fornications, murders, thefts, covetousness, wickedness, deceit, lewdness, an evil eye, blasphemy, pride, foolishness. All these evil things come from within and defile a man." (Mark 7:20-23, NKJV)

But now you yourselves are to put off all these: Anger, wrath, malice, blasphemy, filthy language out of your mouth. Do not lie to one another, since you have put off the old man with his deeds, and have put on the new man who is renewed in knowledge according to the image of Him who created him, (Colossians 3:8-10, NKJV)

And everyone who speaks a word against the Son of Man will be forgiven, but anyone who blasphemes against the Holy Spirit will not be forgiven. (Luke 12:10)

CHAPTER SIX

The "it" of Unbelief

DEFINITION: The biblical meaning of unbelief is refusing to believe in God and His Word. Unbelief is a lack of faith.

FACTS ABOUT UNBELIEF:

The Bible says you are a fool if you do not believe in God. *"The fool says in his heart, "'There is no God'" (Psalm 14:1).*

Some people refuse to be convinced. Jesus said that if people would not listen to the Moses and the prophets, then they would not believe even if someone rose from the dead to confirm the reality of God and His Word (Luke 16:31). Even supernatural miracles will not convince someone who refuses to be convinced (John 4:48).

If you do not believe in God, you are condemned. Jesus said, *"Whoever does not believe stands condemned already because he has not believed in the name of God's one and only Son" (John 3:18).*

Unbelief hinders you from receiving God's promises. You may believe in God, but if you are filled with unbelief regarding the promises in His Word you will miss many great spiritual blessings. God promised Israel their land, but their unbelief kept them from claiming it for forty years! They could not enter in because of their unbelief (Hebrews 3:19).

Unbelief hinders the work of God. Jesus did not do miracles in Nazareth because of their unbelief (Matthew 13:58).

If you deny Christ, He will deny you. *"Whoever acknowledges me before men, I will also acknowledge him before my Father in heaven. But whoever disowns me before men, I will disown him before my Father in heaven" (Matthew 10:32-33).*

DEALING WITH UNBELIEF:

Examine reasons for unbelief. What caused you to reject God and His Word? Perhaps it was disappointment because of unanswered prayer or a great tragedy you experienced. Perhaps you received false teaching. Go to the root cause of your unbelief.

Recognize the vital importance of believing in God and His Word. Your eternal destiny is at stake: *"Whoever believes in the Son has eternal life, but whoever rejects the Son will not see life, for God's wrath remains on him" (John 3:36).* Revelation 21:8 says those who refuse to believe will be separated from God for eternity.

Confess unbelief as sin. Whatever is not of faith is sin (Romans 14:23). Confess your unbelief to God and ask forgiveness.

Ask God to help you believe. As the father who brought his ailing child to Jesus, cry out by faith: *"Lord, I believe. Help me overcome my unbelief!" (Mark 9:24)*.

Study the Word, pray, and fellowship with believers. These three basics will strengthen your core beliefs in God and His Word. Faith comes by the Word of God, and fellowship with other believers strengthens it (Romans 10:17; Hebrews 3:12-13).

WHAT GOD'S WORD SAYS ABOUT UNBELIEF:

The fool says in his heart, "There is no God." (Psalm 14:1)

Those who turn away from you will be written in the dust because they have forsaken the Lord, the spring of living water. (Jeremiah 17:13)

Whoever acknowledges me before men, I will also acknowledge him before my Father in heaven. But whoever disowns me before men, I will disown him before my Father in heaven. (Matthew 10:32-33)

Now He did not do many mighty works there because of their unbelief. (Matthew 13:58)

Then the disciples came to Jesus privately and said, "Why could we not cast it out?" So Jesus said to them, "Because of your unbelief; for assuredly, I say to you, if you have faith as a mustard seed, you will say to this mountain, 'Move from here to there,' and it will move; and nothing will be impossible for you. " (Matthew 17:19-21, NKJV)

"Lord, I believe. Help me overcome my unbelief!" (Mark 9:24).

Later He appeared to the eleven as they sat at the table; and He rebuked their unbelief and hardness of heart, because they did not believe those who had seen Him after He had risen. (Mark 15:14, NKJV)

If they do not listen to Moses and the Prophets, they will not be convinced even if someone rises from the dead. (Luke 16:31)

If you are the Christ," they said, "tell us." Jesus answered, If I tell you, you will not believe me, and if I asked you, you would not answer. (Luke 22:67-68)

Yet to all who received him, to those who believed in his name, he gave the right to become children of God--children born not of natural descent, nor of human decision or a husband's will, but born of God. (John 1:12-13)

Whoever does not believe stands condemned already because he has not believed in the name of God's one and only Son. (John 3:18)

Whoever believes in the Son has eternal life, but whoever rejects the Son will not see life, for God's wrath remains on him. (John 3:36)

Unless you people see miraculous signs and wonders, Jesus told him, you will never believe. (John 4:48)

You diligently study the Scriptures because you think that by them you possess eternal life. These are the Scriptures that testify about me, yet you refuse to come to me to have life. (John 5:39-40)

The words I have spoken to you are spirit and they are life. Yet there are some of you who do not believe. (John 6:63)

For even his own brothers did not believe in him. (John 7:5)

I told you that you would die in your sins; if you do not believe that I am [the one I claim to be], you will indeed die in your sins. (John 8:24)

Can any of you prove me guilty of sin? If I am telling the truth, why don't you believe me? (John 8:46)

Even after Jesus had done all these miraculous signs in their presence, they still would not believe in him. (John 12:37)

They replied, "Believe in the Lord Jesus, and you will be saved--you and your household." (Acts 16:31)

Yet he *(Abraham)* did not waver through unbelief regarding the promise of God, but was strengthened in his faith and gave glory to God, being fully persuaded that God had power to do what he had promised. (Romans 4:20-21)

That if you confess with your mouth, "Jesus is Lord," and believe in your heart that God raised him from the dead, you will be saved. For it is with your heart that you believe and are justified, and it is with your mouth that you confess and are saved. (Romans 10:9-10)

Consequently, faith comes from hearing the message, and the message is heard through the word of Christ. (Romans 10:17)

See to it, brothers, that none of you has a sinful, unbelieving heart that turns away from the living God. But encourage one another daily, as long as it is called Today, so that none of you may be hardened by sin's deceitfulness. (Hebrews 3:12-13)

So, we see that they were not able to enter, because of their unbelief. (Hebrews 3:19)

And without faith it is impossible to please God, because anyone who comes to him must believe that he exists and that he rewards those who earnestly seek him. (Hebrews 11:6)

And this is his command: to believe in the name of his Son, Jesus Christ, and to love one another as he commanded us. (1 John 3:23)

But the cowardly, the unbelieving, the vile, the murderers, the sexually immoral, those who practice magic arts, the idolaters and all liars--their place will be in the fiery lake of burning sulfur. This is the second death.   (Revelation 21:8)

CHAPTER SEVEN

"The "it" of Occults

DEFINITION: The word "occult" means to "hide or conceal a thing." Cults are organized groups of people who participate in phenomena that is satanically originated. Cults hide and conceal these evil practices behind the cloak of religion. Sometimes they even worship Satan and demons.

FACTS ABOUT THE OCCULT:

The occult is real. Its power is derived from Satan.

The occult has many Satanically-inspired practices. These include astrology and horoscopes which use stars to predict events and give guidance, Ouija boards, levitation, astral projection, and séances. Reading of tea leaves, tarot cards, pictures, bumps on the head, palms of the hand and crystal balls are occult practices used for guidance. Witchcraft is part of the occult--using spells, potions, charms, magic, rituals, séances, divinations, methods of chance, divining rods, visions, drawings, and similar unscriptural methods of guidance. Shamanism, Santeria, New Age, mystics, gurus, and communication with the dead are all part of the occult. As a believer, you are to look to the Lord for guidance, not occult practices like astrology, fortune telling, reading palms or tea leaves (Psalm 37:23; Isaiah 30:21).

You need not fear the occult. If you are a believer, walking in fellowship with God, and not dabbling in Satanic rituals and practices, then the occult holds no power over you (1 John 4:4; Luke 10:19).

Participating in the occult is sin. God warned Israel to avoid every type of Satanic influence. He said to *"...destroy all their pictures, and destroy all their molten images, and quite pluck down all their high places" (Numbers 33:52).* Read the additional instructions in Deuteronomy 18:9-14. God's people were to have no contact with the work of Satan in any form.

DEALING WITH THE OCCULT:

Pray for forgiveness for participating in the occult. God expressly forbids participating in such practices. It is sin.

Verbally renounce the occult. Renounce any evil oaths you have made and your allegiance and participation in demonic practices.

Destroy anything that relates to the occult. This would include idols, lucky charms, potions, amulets, crystal balls, games, divining devices, and other similar items. This is what people did in the New Testament when they became believers (Acts 19:19). Destroy any evil literature, music, movies, games, etc.

Do not spend time in places where there is demonic influence. The Bible records that God manifested Himself in special places such as in the temple and the upper room of a house on the

37

Day of Pentecost. It is equally true that Satanic power is manifested in places dedicated to evil. This would include places where evil pictures are shown, drinking and riotous behavior is occurring, séances are being held, worship of Satan is occurring--anywhere sinful practices are going on. Avoid such environments, because Satan's power is especially strong there. You cannot pray the Lord's prayer, "Lead me not into temptation" and then deliberately put yourself in such a place. Do not associate with leaders, teachers, prophets, or ministers of the occult (1 Corinthians 10:20).

Bind the spirits of the occult so that they can no longer operate. Jesus said: *"I tell you the truth, whatever you bind on earth will be bound in heaven, and whatever you loose on earth will be loosed in heaven" (Matthew 18:18).*

Avoid anything related to the occult. This includes literature, movies, music, rituals, objects, and fellowship with others in the occult.

Establish habits of prayer and study of God's Word. To avoid being deceived by occult teachings and practices, examine all you hear in light of God's Word. Be like the Bereans of New Testament times who "...*were more noble than those in Thessalonica, in that they received the Word with all readiness of mind, and searched the Scriptures daily, whether those things were so" (Acts 17:11).* Through regular prayer and Bible study, demonic powers will be broken over your life.

Reject any doctrine that is not in the Word of God. The Apostle Paul warned: *"...but there be some that trouble you and would pervert the Gospel of Christ. But though we or an angel from Heaven preach any other gospel unto you than that which we have preached unto you, let him be accursed" (Galatians 1:7-8).*

WHAT GOD'S WORD SAYS ABOUT THE OCCULT:

Do not practice divination or sorcery. (Leviticus 19:26)

Do not turn to mediums or seek out spiritualist, for you will be defiled by them. I am the Lord your God. (Leviticus 19:31)

I will set my face against the person who turns to mediums and spiritualist to prostitute himself by following them, and I will cut him off from his people. (Leviticus 20:6)

Destroy all their carved images and their cast idols, and demolish all their high places. (Numbers 33:52)

Let no one be found among you who sacrifices his son or daughter in the fire, who practices divination or sorcery, interprets omens, engages in witchcraft, or casts spells, or who is a medium or spiritualist or who consults the dead. Anyone who does these things is detestable to the Lord. (Deuteronomy 18:10-12)

When men tell you to consult mediums and spiritualist, who whisper and mutter, should not a people inquire of their God? Why consult the dead-on behalf of the living? (Isaiah 8:19)

Whether you turn to the right or to the left, your ears will hear a voice behind you, saying, "This is the way; walk in it." Then you will defile your idols overlaid with silver and your images covered with gold; you will throw them away like a menstrual cloth and say to them, "Away with you!" (Isaiah 30:21-22)

Let your astrologers come forward, those stargazers who make predictions month by month, let them save you from what is coming upon you. (Isaiah 47:13)

So, do not listen to your *(false)* prophets, your diviners, your interpreters of dreams, your mediums or your sorcerers... (Jeremiah 27:9)

No wise man, enchanter, magician or diviner can explain to the king the mystery he has asked about, but there is a God in heaven who reveals mysteries. (Daniel 2:27-28)

I will destroy your witchcraft and you will no longer cast spells. (Micah 5:12)

"I tell you the truth, whatever you bind on earth will be bound in heaven, and whatever you loose on earth will be loosed in heaven." (Matthew 18:18)

I have given you authority to trample on snakes and scorpions and to overcome all the power of the enemy; nothing will harm you. (Luke 10: 19)

Many of those who believed now came and openly confessed their evil deeds. A number who had practiced sorcery brought their scrolls together and burned them publicly. When they calculated the value of the scrolls, the total came to fifty thousand drachmas. In this way the word of the Lord spread widely and grew in power. (Acts 19:18-20)

...I do not want you to be participants with demons. You cannot drink the cup of the Lord and the cup of demons too; you cannot have a part in both the Lord's table and the table of demons. (1 Corinthians 10:20-21)

But even if we or an angel from heaven should preach a gospel other than the one we preached to you, let him be eternally condemned! As we have already said, so now I say again: If anybody is preaching to you a gospel other than what you accepted, let him be eternally condemned! (Galatians 1:8-9)

The acts of the sinful nature are obvious: sexual immorality, impurity and debauchery; idolatry and witchcraft; hatred, discord, jealousy, fits of rage, selfish ambition, dissensions, factions and envy; drunkenness, orgies, and the like. I warn you, as I did before, that those who live like this will not inherit the kingdom of God. (Galatians 5:19-21)

Command certain men not to teach false doctrines any longer nor to devote themselves to myths and endless genealogies. These promote controversies rather than God's work--which is by faith. (1 Timothy 1:3-4)

Have nothing to do with godless myths and old wives' tales; rather, train yourselves to be godly. (1 Timothy 4:7)

You, dear children, are from God and have overcome them, because the one who is in you is greater than the one who is in the world. (1 John 4:4)

They did not stop worshiping demons, and idols of gold, silver, bronze, stone and wood --idols that cannot see or hear or walk. Nor did they repent of their murders, their magic arts, their sexual immorality or their thefts. (Revelation 9:20-21)

But the cowardly, the unbelieving, the vile, the murderers, the sexually immoral, those who practice magic arts, the idolaters and all liars--their place will be in the fiery lake of burning sulfur. This is the second death. (Revelation 21:8)

Outside are... those who practice magic arts, the sexually immoral, the murderers, the idolaters and everyone who loves and practices falsehood. (Revelation 22:15)

CHAPTER EIGHT

The "it" of Idolatry

DEFINITION: Idolatry is the worship of idols and false gods. Idolatry includes putting anything before the one true and living God who is revealed in the Holy Bible. This also includes excessive adoration of a person, obsession with an activity, money, or materialism.

FACTS ABOUT IDOLATRY:

Idolatry is sin. The first of the ten commandments is *"You shall have no other gods before me. You shall not make for yourself* an idol *in the form of anything in heaven above or on the earth beneath or in the waters below." (Exodus 20:3).* Idolatry is also listed as one of the works of the flesh (acts of the sinful nature) in Galatians 5:19-20 and in Colossians 3:5.

Idolatry is more than just worshiping an idol. It is any commitment to a person or group of people, activities, or material things that you put before God--you love these more than you love God.

Proud and arrogant behavior is idolatry. The Bible says*: "For rebellion is like the sin of divination, and arrogance like the evil of idolatry" (1 Samuel 15:23).* When you are rebellious and arrogant, you are establishing yourself as an idol! Deciding to do it "your way" instead of God's way is rebellion and is compared to the sins of witchcraft and idolatry.

Materialism is idolatry. Money in itself is not wrong, but the Bible says that the love of money is the root of all evil (1 Timothy 6:10). Those who worship money and material things err from the faith and experience many sorrows.

You cannot worship God and still worship an idol. Dualism in worship is idolatry because God is not in first place and is not receiving your total allegiance and worship (Matthew 6:24). Any form of idolatry estranges you from God (Ezekiel 14:5). You cannot be a temple for both God and idols (2 Corinthians 6:16).

Doing things because "everyone else is doing them" is idolatry. The Lord said that Israel imitated the sinful nations around them, although God had ordered them not to do so. They followed idolatrous people and became idolatrous themselves (2 Kings 17:15). When you decide to do something because "everyone else is doing it", you are establishing those people as an idol- -imitating them and adhering to their standards instead of following God.

You are not to keep company with idolaters. This does not mean you cannot minister to them, but that they should not be your close friends (1 Corinthians 5:11).

Those who worship idols will become as worthless as their idols (2 Kings 17:15) and be put to shame (Psalm 97:7). They will become like the idols they worship (Psalms 115:4-8).

41

Idols have no power. They are made by men and are powerless to aid you in times of trouble (Psalms 115:4-8). Idolatry--the worship of idols--is very powerful however. It is a practice that has drawn many to serve false gods.

Idolaters will not inherit the Kingdom of God. *"Do you not know that the wicked will not inherit the kingdom of God? Do not be deceived: Neither the sexually immoral nor* idolaters ... *" (1 Corinthians 6:9-10).* The destination of idolaters is the lake of fire (Revelation 21:8).

How to recognize idolatrous behavior. Bowing down before an idol, making one, praying to one, and using items designated for worship of an idol are immediately recognizable as idolatry but idolatry also includes anything or anyone that consumes your passion, your thoughts, and your time more than serving God. Things that in themselves are not wrong--like a hobby or an activity--can become an idol in your life if these things become more important than your commitment to God. Ezekiel 14:3-4 speaks of "idols in the heart"--meaning anything in your heart that comes before God.

DEALING WITH IDOLATRY:

Repent of idolatry. Idolatry is sin and, as in the case of all sins, you must confess and repent of it. Repent of any rebellious, proud, or arrogant behavior. When you do, God has promised: *"I will sprinkle clean water on you, and you will be clean; I will cleanse you from all your impurities and from all your idols." (Ezekiel 36:25).* He also promised that you...*"will no longer defile themselves with their idols and vile images or with any of their offenses, for I will save them from all their sinful backsliding, and I will cleanse them. They will be my people, and I will be their God" (Ezekiel 37:23).* Ask God to forgive you if you have put a person, an activity, or material things before God.

Determine you will worship and serve only the true God. There is only one true God, and that is the God revealed in the Holy Bible which is His Word (1 Corinthians 8:4-6).

Eliminate idolatrous objects. These include any idols, charms, books, music, or other items used to worship of false gods. Eliminate posters and pictures of performers, movie stars, and sports heroes--anyone you have idolized before God (Exodus 23:24).

Foster a new love for God. Your love will grow by spending time with God in prayer and worship, studying the Word, and by attending a Bible-believing church.

Keep your focus on God instead of the things of the world. All that is in the world--including your idols--will pass away: *"Do not love the world or anything in the world. If anyone loves the world, the love of the Father is not in him. For everything in the world--the cravings of sinful man, the lust of his eyes and the boasting of what he has and does--comes not from the Father but from the world. The world and its desires pass away, but the man who does the will of God lives forever" (1 John 2:15-17).*

Keep yourself from idols. The Bible cautions: *"Dear children, keep yourselves from idols" (1 John 5:21).* You can keep yourself from idolatrous behavior by immersing yourself in God's Word and refraining from participating in any activity that draws you away from His plan and purposes for your life. Things that in themselves are not wrong--like a hobby or an activity--may be wrong for you if it becomes an idol in your life. It is your responsibility to eliminate these things. The Bible commands you to put idolatry to death (Colossians 3:5-6).

WHAT GOD'S WORD SAYS ABOUT IDOLATRY:

You shall have no other gods before me. You shall not make for yourself an idol in the form of anything in heaven above or on the earth beneath or in the waters below. You shall not bow down to them or worship them; for I, the Lord your God, am a jealous God, punishing the children for the sin of the fathers to the third and fourth generation of those who hate me, but showing love to a thousand [generations] of those who love me and keep my commandments. (Exodus 20:3-6)

Do not make any gods to be alongside me; do not make for yourselves gods of silver or gods of gold. (Exodus 20:23)

Do not bow down before their gods or worship them or follow their practices. You must demolish them and break their sacred stones to pieces. (Exodus 23:24)

Do not turn to idols or make gods of cast metal for yourselves. I am the Lord your God. (Leviticus 19:4)

Do not make idols or set up an image or a sacred stone for yourselves, and do not place a carved stone in your land to bow down before it. I am the Lord your God. (Leviticus 26:1)

Make sure there is no man or woman, clan or tribe among you today whose heart turns away from the Lord our God to go and worship the gods of those nations; make sure there is no root among you that produces such bitter poison. (Deuteronomy 29:18. See also through verse 29)

Do not turn away after useless idols. They can do you no good, nor can they rescue you, because they are useless. (1 Samuel 12:21)

For rebellion is like the sin of divination, and arrogance like the evil of idolatry. (1 Samuel 15:23)

They rejected his decrees and the covenant he had made with their fathers and the warnings he had given them. They followed worthless idols and themselves became worthless. They imitated the nations around them although the Lord had ordered them, "Do not do as they do," and they did the things the Lord had forbidden them to do. (2 Kings 17:15)

They would not listen, however, but persisted in their former practices. Even while these people were worshipping the Lord, they were serving their idols. To this day their children and grandchildren continue to do as their fathers did. (1 Kings 17:40-41)

For all the gods of the nations are idols, but the Lord made the heavens. (Psalm 96:5)

All who worship images are put to shame, those who boast in idols... (Psalm 97:7)

But their idols are silver and gold, made by the hands of men. They have mouths, but cannot speak, eyes, but they cannot see; they have ears, but cannot hear, noses, but they cannot smell; they have hands, but cannot feel, feet, but they cannot walk; nor can they utter a sound with their throats. Those who make them will be like them, and so will all who trust in them. (Psalms 115:4-8)

And the idols he shall utterly abolish... (Isaiah 2:18)

"I am the Lord; that is my name! I will not give my glory to another or my praise to idols." (Isaiah 42:8)

I will expose your righteousness and your works, and they will not benefit you. When you cry out for help, let your collection [of idols] save you! The wind will carry all of them off, a mere breath will blow them away. But the man who makes me his refuge will inherit the land and possess my holy mountain." (Isaiah 57:12)

This is what the Lord says: "What fault did your fathers find in me, that they strayed so far from me? They followed worthless idols and became worthless themselves." (Jeremiah 2:5)

How I have been grieved by their adulterous hearts, which have turned away from me, and by their eyes, which have lusted after their idols. They will loathe themselves for the evil they have done and for all their detestable practices." (Ezekiel 6:8-9)

"I will sprinkle clean water on you, and you will be clean; I will cleanse you from all your impurities and from all your idols." (Ezekiel 36:25)

"They will no longer defile themselves with their idols and vile images or with any of their offenses, for I will save them from all their sinful backsliding, and I will cleanse them. They will be my people, and I will be their God." (Ezekiel 37:23)

Of what value is an idol, since a man has carved it? Or an image that teaches lies? For he who makes it trusts in his own creation; he makes idols that cannot speak. Woe to him who says to wood, 'Come to life!' Or to lifeless stone, 'Wake up!' Can it give guidance? It is covered with gold and silver; there is no breath in it. (Habakkuk 2:18-19)

No one can serve two masters. Either he will hate the one and love the other, or he will be devoted to the one and despise the other. You cannot serve both God and Money. (Matthew 6:24)

But now I am writing you that you must not associate with anyone who calls himself a brother
but is sexually immoral or greedy, an idolater or a slanderer, a drunkard or a swindler. With such
a man do not even eat. (1 Corinthians 5:11)

Do you not know that the wicked will not inherit the kingdom of God? Do not be deceived:
Neither the sexually immoral nor idolaters ... (1 Corinthians 6:9-10)

So then, about eating food sacrificed to idols: We know that an idol is nothing at all in the world
and that there is no God but one. For even if there are so-called gods, whether in heaven or on
earth (as indeed there are many "gods" and many "lords"), yet for us there is but one God, the
Father, from whom all things came and for whom we live; and there is but one Lord, Jesus
Christ, through whom all things came and through whom we live. (1 Corinthians 8:4-6)

Do not be idolaters, as some of them were; as it is written: "The people sat down to eat and drink
and got up to indulge in pagan revelry." (1 Corinthians 10:7)

Therefore, my dear friends, flee from idolatry. (1 Corinthians 10:14)

Do I mean then that a sacrifice offered to an idol is anything, or that an idol is anything? No, but
the sacrifices of pagans are offered to demons, not to God, and I do not want you to be
participants with demons. You cannot drink the cup of the Lord and the cup of demons too; you
cannot have a part in both the Lord's table and the table of demons. (1 Corinthians 10:19-21)

...I do not wish you to be ignorant... somehow or other you were influenced and led astray to
dumb idols. (1 Corinthians 12:1-2)

What agreement is there between the temple of God and idols? For we are the temple of the
living God. As God has said: "I will live with them and walk among them, and I will be their
God, and they will be my people. Therefore come out from them and be separate, says the
Lord. Touch no unclean thing, and I will receive you. I will be a Father to you,
and you will be my sons and daughters, says the Lord Almighty."   (2 Corinthians 6:16-18)

The acts of the sinful nature are obvious: sexual immorality, impurity and debauchery; idolatry
and witchcraft; hatred, discord, jealousy, fits of rage, selfish ambition, dissensions, factions and
envy; drunkenness, orgies, and the like. I warn you, as I did before, that those who live like this
will not inherit the kingdom of God. (Galatians 5:19-20)

For of this you can be sure: No immoral, impure or greedy person--such a man is an idolater--has
any inheritance in the kingdom of Christ and of God. (Ephesians 5:5)

Put to death, therefore, whatever belongs to your earthly nature: sexual immorality, impurity,
lust, evil desires and greed, which is idolatry. (Colossians 3:5-6)

...They tell how you turned to God from idols to serve the living and true God, (1 Thessalonians
1:9)

For the love of money is a root of all kinds of evil. Some people, eager for money, have wandered from the faith and pierced themselves with many griefs. (1 Timothy 6:10)

Do not love the world or anything in the world. If anyone loves the world, the love of the Father is not in him. For everything in the world--the cravings of sinful man, the lust of his eyes and the boasting of what he has and does--comes not from the Father but from the world. The world and its desires pass away, but the man who does the will of God lives forever. (1 John 2:15-17)

Dear children, keep yourselves from idols. (1 John 5:21)

But the cowardly, the unbelieving, the vile, the murderers, the sexually immoral, those who practice magic arts, the idolaters and all liars--their place will be in the fiery lake of burning sulfur. This is the second death. (Revelation 21:8)

CHAPTER NINE

The "it" of Curses

DEFINITION: Curses are powerful forces that operate in the spiritual realm.   A curse--also sometimes referred to as a jinx, hex, or execration--is any expressed wish that some sort of adversity or misfortune will befall a person. It can also be a command for evil powers to attach themselves to a certain place or object.

FACTS ABOUT CURSES:

Curses are not primitive superstitions. Curses are mentioned over 200 times in Scripture. People in the western world are not as aware of the power of curses as people in nations where witchcraft, Wicca, and Shamanism are common--but they are strong spiritual forces that cannot be ignored.

Both blessings and curses are invisible forces of spiritual power which are transmitted by words (Proverbs 18:21). You can speak positive words of blessing over someone, or negative words of curses that cause despair, discouragement, and destruction in a person's life.

The first instance of blessing and curses is found in Genesis. God blessed mankind (Genesis 1:28). In Genesis 3, due to the entrance of sin into the world, the first curses result. Curses are always linked in some way to a violation of God's Word--either by the person themselves or by a person who is putting a curse on someone.

Curses have causes. The Bible says *"...the curse causeless shall not come" (Proverbs 26:2)*, meaning there is always a root cause behind a curse. Curses can result from witchcraft and the occult, of course, but they also arise from:
> -Having false gods: Exodus 20:3- 4; Deuteronomy 27: 15.
> -Disrespect for parents: Deuteronomy 27:16.
> -Treachery against a neighbor: Deuteronomy 27: 17.
> -Committing injustices: Deuteronomy 27: 18-19.
> -Sexual sins: Deuteronomy 27: 20-23.
> -Lying: Deuteronomy 27: 25.
> -Stealing: Zechariah 5:1-4.
> -Robbing God: Malachi 3: 9.
> -Perverting the gospel: Galatians 1:8- 9.
> -Depending on the flesh instead of God: Jeremiah 17:5.
> -Acts of racial discrimination: Genesis 12:3, Genesis 28:3 and 14.

Self-imposed curses result when you make declarations like: "I'll never be any good. I am so stupid. God doesn't love me. I hate myself. I will never forgive myself. No one cares. I am better off dead. "You are actually putting a curse on yourself by your own words.

Curses imposed by others--authority figures in your life, your spouse, your parents, etc.-- include statements such as "You are no good, you are useless, you are stupid, you are a failure, you will never achieve anything, you are ugly." Curses can also be imposed by those engaged in witchcraft and from maintaining relationships with those engaged in such satanic practices.

Generational curses are negative spiritual traits passed down from a previous generation. These are sinful spiritual strongholds that have controlled the attitudes and actions of your ancestors. In the natural world it is possible to have a propensity towards certain physical conditions--cancer, heart disease, diabetes, etc.--due to heredity. The same is true in the spiritual world. For example, if your ancestors were involved in the occult, you may have a predisposition to dabble in it also and/or you may be affected by it. Chronic sickness can be a generational curse passed down from your ancestors, as well as a tendency to use addictive substances. Children often repeat the sins of their parents. Through your sin, you can erect spiritual strongholds that will be passed on as generational curses to your children and succeeding generations. You can also pass on spiritual blessings. Just as curses can be passed to a succeeding generation, so can blessings (Deuteronomy 5:8-10 and Psalm 103:17).

Curses can be broken through the blood of Jesus. Galatians 3:13 confirms that: *"Christ redeemed us from the curse of the law by becoming a curse for us, for it is written: "Cursed is everyone who is hung on a tree."* Jesus not only redeemed you from sin when He died at Calvary, but He also redeemed you from every curse.

DEALING WITH CURSES:

Recognize the signs of a curse operating in your life. Your life may seem to get increasingly harder. You may experience constant hardships, frustration, poverty, or be unproductive in your labors. You may live in continual defeat or experience chronic mental, emotional, or physical problems. Barrenness and being accident-prone are also signs of a curse.

Recognize that you have the power to choose either blessings or curses. God told Israel: *"See, I am setting before you today a blessing and a curse--the blessing if you obey the commands of the Lord your God that I am giving you today; the curse if you disobey the commands of the Lord your God and turn from the way that I command you today by following other gods, which you have not known" (Deuteronomy 11:26-28).* You do not have to be a victim of curses.

Go to the root cause of curses. The Bible says *"...the curse causeless shall not come" (Proverbs 26:2),* meaning there is always a root cause behind a curse. Curses can result from witchcraft and the occult, of course, but you can also operate under a curse because of your own words and sins. See the causes of curses in the previous section. Cut the root and you will kill the fruit!

Acknowledge your sin. Acknowledge your sin and take personal responsibility for any sinful practices in which you are engaged. Confess and repent of these sins (Ezekiel 18:20). Freeing yourself from the results of your own sinful behavior is the first step in breaking curses. For example, if you are participating in a cult, a curse may be on you because of your participation. Idolatry opens the door to spiritual curses, as does sexual immorality and deliberate disobedience to God and His Word.

Identify generational curses. If you are struggling with issues passed down from your parents--and if your siblings also struggle in these areas--you most likely are living under a generational curse.

Break every curse in the name of Jesus. A stronghold is an area in your life where the enemy has established control. It may be a hold he has over your attitudes, behaviors, emotions, or your finances. The Bible declares that you have power over all the power of the enemy (Luke 10:19). Claim the power of the blood of Jesus and take authority over Satan in every area of your life. Pray a prayer of deliverance, binding the power of Satan and breaking every curse or generational curse operating in your life. Here is a sample prayer: *"In the name of Jesus, I confess my sins and break any curses operating in my life. The strongholds of curses have no hold over my life. In the name of Jesus, and by the power of His blood, I declare that every curse is broken over my life. I am no longer in bondage and I declare myself to be free from all curses."*

Put on the spiritual armor of God. Study Ephesians 6:10-21 and the topic of "Spiritual Warfare" in this database. The armor of God will protect you against curses.

Refuse to engage in curse-causing behavior. Things like rebellion, negative emotions, witchcraft, the occult, addictive substances, and sexual sins all can result in spiritual curses in your life.

Destroy objects associated with the occult--things associated with idolatry, witchcraft, books, charms, tarot cards, games, etc. Break relationships with people involved in the occult or witchcraft.

WHAT GOD'S WORD SAYS ABOUT CURSES:

You shall not make for yourself an idol in the form of anything in heaven above or on the earth beneath or in the waters below. You shall not bow down to them or worship them; for I, the Lord your God, am a jealous God, punishing the children for the sin of the fathers to the third and fourth generation of those who hate me, but showing love to a thousand [generations] of those who love me and keep my commandments. (Deuteronomy 5:8-10)

See, I am setting before you today a blessing and a curse--the blessing if you obey the commands of the Lord your God that I am giving you today; the curse if you disobey the commands of the Lord your God and turn from the way that I command you today by following other gods, which you have not known. (Deuteronomy 11:26-18)

But from everlasting to everlasting the Lord's love is with those who fear him, and his righteousness with their children's children--with those who keep his covenant and remember to obey his precepts. (Psalm 103:17-18)

The tongue has the power of life and death, and those who love it will eat its fruit.

(Proverbs 18:21)

...the curse causeless shall not come. (Proverbs 26:2)

In those days people will no longer say, 'The fathers have eaten sour grapes and the children's teeth are set on edge.' Instead, everyone will die for his own sin; whoever eats sour grapes--his own teeth will be set on edge. (Jeremiah 31:29-30)

You show love to thousands but bring the punishment for the fathers' sins into the laps of their children after them. O great and powerful God, whose name is the Lord Almighty, great are your purposes and mighty are your deeds. Your eyes are open to all the ways of men; you reward everyone according to his conduct and as his deeds deserve. (Jeremiah 32:18-19)

So, if the Son sets you free, you will be free indeed. (John 8:36)

Therefore, if anyone is in Christ, he is a new creation; old things have passed away; behold, all things have become new. (2 Corinthians 5:17)

Christ redeemed us from the curse of the law by becoming a curse for us, for it is written: "Cursed is everyone who is hung on a tree." (Galatians 3:13)

CHAPTER TEN

The "it" of Generational Curses

DEFINITION: Generational curses are spiritual bondages or predispositions for sinful behaviors that are passed down from one generation to another.

FACTS ABOUT GENERATIONAL CURSES:

Natural heredity is a term used to describe how living organisms reproduce after their kind. It concerns the presence or absence of certain characteristics--physical, emotional, and personality traits that are passed biologically from one generation to another.

Spiritual heredity refers to spiritual blessings or curses that are passed from one generation to the next. Spiritual heredity--what you received spiritually from your ancestors--can be either positive or negative in your life. You may have had godly parents who gave you a good spiritual heritage, or you may have had unsaved parents who were hostile, angry, and addicted and passed some of these issues on to you.

Blessing and cursing are invisible forces of spiritual power which are transmitted by words (Proverbs 18:21). You can speak positive words of blessing over someone, or negative words of curses that cause despair, discouragement, and destruction in a person's life.

Generational curses are negative spiritual traits passed down from a previous generation. These are sinful spiritual strongholds that have controlled the attitudes and actions of your ancestors. In the natural world it is possible to have a propensity towards certain physical conditions--cancer, heart disease, diabetes, etc.--due to heredity. The same is true in the spiritual world. For example, if your ancestors were involved in the occult, you may have a predisposition to dabble in it also and you may be affected by it. Chronic sickness can be a generational curse passed down from your ancestors, as well as a tendency to use addictive substances. Children often repeat the sins of their parents.

You can initiate and pass on curses to following generations. Through your personal sin, you can erect spiritual strongholds that will be passed on to your children and succeeding generations.

Generational curses can be broken through the blood of Jesus. Galatians 3:13 says *"Christ redeemed us from the curse of the law by becoming a curse for us, for it is written: "Cursed is everyone who is hung on a tree."* Jesus not only redeemed you from sin when He died at Calvary, but He also redeemed you from every curse.

You can pass on spiritual blessings. Just as curses can be passed to succeeding generations, so can blessings. See Deuteronomy 5:8-10 and Psalm 103:17.

51

DEALING WITH GENERATIONAL CURSES:

Acknowledge known sin. Acknowledge your sin and take personal responsibility for any sinful practices in which you are engaged. Confess and repent of these sins (Ezekiel 18:20).

Identify generational curses. If you are struggling with issues passed down from your parents-- and if your siblings also struggle in these areas--you most likely are living under a generational curse.

Break every curse in the name of Jesus. A stronghold is an area in your life where the enemy has established control. It may be a hold he has over your attitudes, behaviors, emotions, or your finances. Claim the power of the blood of Jesus and take authority over Satan in every area of your life. Pray a prayer of deliverance, binding the power of Satan and breaking any curses or generational spirits operating in your life. Here is a sample prayer: *"In the name of Jesus, I confess the sins and iniquities of my ancestors and declare that these strongholds have no hold over my life. In the name of Jesus, and by the power of His blood, I declare that every generational curse is broken over my life. I am no longer in bondage and I declare myself and future generations freed from bondages passed down by our ancestors."*

Refuse to engage in curse-causing behavior. Things like rebellion, negative emotions, witchcraft, the occult, addictive substances, and sexual sins all result in spiritual curses in your life. Reject such behaviors so that you do not erect spiritual strongholds and pass curses on to your descendants.

WHAT GOD'S WORD SAYS ABOUT GENERATIONAL CURSES:

And he passed in front of Moses, proclaiming, "The Lord, the Lord, the compassionate and gracious God, slow to anger, abounding in love and faithfulness, maintaining love to thousands, and forgiving wickedness, rebellion and sin. Yet he does not leave the guilty unpunished; he punishes the children and their children for the sin of the fathers to the third and fourth generation." (Exodus 34:6-7)

The Lord is slow to anger, abounding in love and forgiving sin and rebellion. Yet he does not leave the guilty unpunished; he punishes the children for the sin of the fathers to the third and fourth generation. (Numbers 14:18)

You shall not make for yourself an idol in the form of anything in heaven above or on the earth beneath or in the waters below. You shall not bow down to them or worship them; for I, the Lord your God, am a jealous God, punishing the children for the sin of the fathers to the third and fourth generation of those who hate me, but showing love to a thousand [generations] of those who love me and keep my commandments. (Deuteronomy 5:8-10)

But from everlasting to everlasting the Lord's love is with those who fear him, and his righteousness with their children's children-- with those who keep his covenant and remember to obey his precepts. (Psalm 103:17-18)

The tongue has the power of life and death, and those who love it will eat its fruit. (Proverbs 18:21)

In those days people will no longer say, 'The fathers have eaten sour grapes and the children's teeth are set on edge.' Instead, everyone will die for his own sin; whoever eats sour grapes--his own teeth will be set on edge. (Jeremiah 31:29-30)

You show love to thousands but bring the punishment for the fathers' sins into the laps of their children after them. O great and powerful God, whose name is the Lord Almighty, great are your purposes and mighty are your deeds. Your eyes are open to all the ways of men; you reward everyone according to his conduct and as his deeds deserve. (Jeremiah 32:18-19)

The soul who sins shall die. The son shall not bear the guilt of the father, nor the father bear the guilt of the son. The righteousness of the righteous shall be upon himself, and the wickedness of the wicked shall be upon himself. (Ezekiel 18:20)

So, if the Son sets you free, you will be free indeed. (John 8:36)

Therefore, if anyone is in Christ, he is a new creation; old things have passed away; behold, all things have become new. (2 Corinthians 5:17)

Christ redeemed us from the curse of the law by becoming a curse for us, for it is written: "Cursed is everyone who is hung on a tree." (Galatians 3:13)

CHAPTER ELEVEN

The "it" of Incest

DEFINITION: Incest is sexual relations between close relatives.

FACTS ABOUT INCEST:

Incest is against the law in many nations. It is punishable by imprisonment and, in some societies, by death.

Incest is sin. Whether or not incest is considered illegal by the society in which you live or whether or not it is consensual, it is sin in God's sight. Leviticus 18:6-18 is very clear about this.

Incest is abuse. Incest is abusive, with one person exercising sexual power over another. Such abuse results in many other problems. For example, sexually abused children often suffer from low self-image, are depressed, and harbor thoughts of suicide. Many runs away from the abusive situation and get involved in addictions and other deviant sexual behaviors such as prostitution and homosexuality.

Incest can result in genetic disorders. Congenital disorders, birth defects, disabilities, and death are caused by inbreeding.

DEALING WITH INCEST:

If you are committing incest--stop it immediately. Admit it as sin and seek forgiveness from God and from the person against whom or with whom you committed this sin. As with all sin, forgiveness is available through Jesus Christ.

If you are presently a victim of incest--tell someone. Tell a trusted friend who can help you escape and/or confront the abuser. If you are underage, tell authorities who have the power to remove you from the situation. Do not be intimidated by family members who do not believe you or do not want you to reveal the truth.

If have been a victim of incest--forgive your abuser and ask God to heal you from the mental, emotional, and physical effects of the abuse. God has promised to heal the brokenhearted (Psalm 147:3). If you were a victim, the incest was not your fault. You were forced to do something degrading and you are not responsible for the wrong that was done to you.

Turn to God's Word and prayer for comfort, healing, and deliverance. Make these practices part of your everyday life. Whether you were a victim of incest or a perpetrator of it, prayer and the Word will heal your pain and change your life.

WHAT GOD'S WORD SAYS ABOUT INCEST:

No one is to approach any close relative to have sexual relations. I am the Lord. Do not dishonor your father by having sexual relations with your mother. She is your mother; do not have relations with her. Do not have sexual relations with your father's wife; that would dishonor your father. Do not have sexual relations with your sister, either your father's daughter or your mother's daughter, whether she was born in the same home or elsewhere. Do not have sexual relations with your son's daughter or your daughter's daughter; that would dishonor you. Do not have sexual relations with the daughter of your father's wife, born to your father; she is your sister. Do not have sexual relations with your father's sister; she is your father's close relative. Do not have sexual relations with your mother's sister, because she is your mother's close relative. Do not dishonor your father's brother by approaching his wife to have sexual relations; she is your aunt. Do not have sexual relations with your daughter-in-law. She is your son's wife; do not have relations with her. Do not have sexual relations with your brother's wife; that would dishonor your brother. Do not have sexual relations with both a woman and her daughter. Do not have sexual relations with either her son's daughter or her daughter's daughter; they are her close relatives. That is wickedness. Do not take your wife's sister as a rival wife and have sexual relations with her while your wife is living. (Leviticus 18:6-18)

If a man marries his sister, the daughter of either his father or his mother, and they have sexual relations, it is a disgrace. They must be cut off before the eyes of their people. He has dishonored his sister and will be held responsible. (Leviticus 20:17)

It is actually reported that there is sexual immorality among you, and of a kind that does not occur even among pagans: A man has his father's wife. And you are proud! Shouldn't you rather have been filled with grief and have put out of your fellowship the man who did this? Even though I am not physically present, I am with you in spirit. And I have already passed judgment on the one who did this, just as if I were present. When you are assembled in the name of our Lord Jesus and I am with you in spirit, and the power of our Lord Jesus is present, hand this man over to Satan, so that the sinful nature may be destroyed and his spirit saved on the day of the Lord. (1 Corinthians 5:1-5)

CHAPTER TWELVE

The "it" of Demons and Deliverance

DEFINITION: Demons are fallen angels who joined Satan's rebellion against God and were cast out of heaven (Revelation 12:7-9). They were originally angels of God but are now evil spirits operating under Satan's control. They are also referred to as "devils", as distinct from the Devil who is Satan. People affected by demons are in need of deliverance from captivity and/or the influence of demonic powers.

FACTS ABOUT DEMONS AND DELIVERANCE:

Spiritual warfare is a battle with the forces of evil, Satan and his hosts of demons (Ephesians 6:12). Our armor is truth, righteousness, the Gospel, faith, and salvation. The Word of God and prayer are powerful spiritual weapons (Ephesians 6:14-18). Our authority and power are from Jesus (Mark 16:17).

How demons operate. Demons oppose God, His plan and purposes, and His people. They also war against unbelievers to keep them from the truth of the Gospel. Demons control specific territories (principalities) such as the prince of Persia mentioned in Daniel 10:12-13. Demons also work through personalities--through men and women--to accomplish Satanic objectives in the world. Opposition to God's will and His Word is Satan's main objective. The word "Satan" means "adversary." Satan and his demonic host are primarily God's adversary (Job 1:6; Matthew 13:39). He is secondarily, man's adversary (Zechariah 3:1; 1 Peter 5:8).

Demons have different natures. One demon identified himself as a "lying spirit" (1 Kings 22:23). A "deaf and dumb" spirit is identified in Mark 9:25. Demons of various natures operate as spirits of infirmity, seducing spirits, and unclean spirits.

> -Spirits of infirmity afflict the bodies of believers as well as unbelievers. See the story of the daughter of Abraham (a Jewish believer) in Luke 13:10-17. For other examples of demonic powers afflicting the body see Matthew 12:22; 17:15-18; Acts 10:38; 1 Corinthians 12:7.

> -Seducing spirits afflict the spirit of man, seducing him to believe doctrinal lies and be condemned to eternal punishment. They are deceptive spirits of false doctrine, cults, false Christs, and false teachers (1 Timothy 4:1). They do miraculous works which lead some to believe they are of God (Revelation 16:14; 2 Thessalonians 2:9-10). Seducing spirits include the "spirit of divination" mentioned in Acts 16:16 and "familiar spirits" that operate in fortune tellers, witches, and palm, crystal ball, and tea leaf readers. Through unscriptural methods of divination, these spirits foretell the future and reveal things not naturally known. Warnings against familiar spirits are given in Leviticus 19:31; 20:6; Deuteronomy 5:9; 18:10; Leviticus 20:27; and 1 Samuel 28:3. Seducing spirits sear the conscience, seduce, entice, tempt, allure, interest, fascinate, excite, arouse, attract, and deceive. They are operative in every cult and wherever doctrinal error exists. Seducing spirits entice men and women to worship idols and even Satan himself.

56

-Unclean spirits afflict the soul. They are responsible for immoral acts and unclean thoughts. When Satan controls individuals with unclean spirits, he uses them to cause problems in homes, churches, and nations. This is how Satan works in the various levels of structure in society (Matthew 10:1; 12:43; Mark 1:23-26).

Demonic oppression. To oppress means to bear down, come against, or bind from the outside. This oppression is accomplished by evil spirits in various ways. They cause depression, create negative circumstances, and cause wrong thoughts such as of suicide, immorality, unbelief, fear, etc.

-A physical binding: The "daughter of Abraham" who Jesus relieved of a spirit of infirmity was bound physically (Luke 13:10-17). Chronic sickness may be demonic oppression, although all illness is not caused by demonic powers.

-A mental oppression: Disturbances in the mind such as mental torment, confusion, doubt, loss of memory, etc. Restlessness, an inability to reason or listen to others, abnormal talkativeness or reserve may be exhibited. All mental problems are not caused by Satan, but some definitely are caused by demonic influence.

-Emotional problems: Disturbances in the emotions which persist or recur, including resentment, hatred, anger, fear, rejection, self-pity, jealousy, depression, worry, insecurity, inferiority, etc.

-Spiritual problems: Extreme difficulties in overcoming sin and sinful habits. Spiritual solutions are rejected and doctrinal error is frequent.

-Circumstances: Demons can create difficult circumstances which are oppressive. These circumstances usually involve confusion and can immediately be identified as demonic because God is not the author of confusion (1 Corinthians 14:33; James 3:16).

Demonic possession. Demon possession is a condition in which one or more evil spirits (demons) inhabit the body of a human being and take complete control of their victim at will. Some people prefer using the word "demonized" rather than possession, but regardless of the term, the possessed person is host to resident demons. "Possession" does not mean a person is not responsible for his own sin. His responsibility rests in the actions that led to his condition, i.e., involvement with demonic influences. Demonic possession can be recognized by the following signs:

-Indwelling of an unclean spirit: This is demonstrated by a basic moral uncleanness and filthiness. For examples see Mark 5:2 and Luke 8:27.

-Unusual physical strength: A person shows strength beyond normal capabilities. For examples see Mark 5:3 and Luke 8:29.

-Fits of rage: See Mark 9:14-29 and Luke 8:26-39.

-Resistance to spiritual things: In the accounts in Mark 6:7 and 1:21-28, the demons knew Jesus and asked Him to leave them alone. Fear of the name of Jesus, prayer, and the Word and blasphemy of that which is spiritual are all symptoms of demon possession.

-Changes in personality and/or voice: A person who is normally shy may become aggressive or violent. Actions as well as appearance may be affected. Moral character and intelligence may change. The voice may be altered (Mark 5:9).

-Accompanying physical afflictions: These appear most commonly as afflictions of the mental and nervous systems (Matthew 9:33; 12:22; Mark 5:4-5). They can also include a general wasting away physically. (Mark 9:14-29).

-Self-inflicted physical injury: In Matthew 17:1421 there is the story of a man's son who would cast himself in the fire. In Luke 8:26-39 this demon possessed man cut himself with stones to inflict physical injury.

-Terrible anguish: Luke 8:28 relates that this man went about crying because of the inner torment caused by his possession.

-Incapacity for normal living: This man could not reside in society, but lived in the tombs of the cemetery (Luke 8:27).

-Divination: This is the ability, through unscriptural methods, to foretell the future or reveal that which is unknown. The woman in Acts 16:16 is said to be possessed by a spirit of divination.

-Obsessive immorality such as involvement with pornography, adultery, fornication, homosexuality, and other sexual sins. Strong compulsions toward eating disorders, suicide, self-mutilation, maiming, and murder.

-Addiction to drugs or alcohol.

-Trances, visions, and meditation which are not focused on or from the one true God.

-Bondage to emotions: Rage, hatred, jealousy, etc.

Demon obsession. This is a condition where one is obsessed by an interest in or preoccupation with demons. It is an unusual interest in the occult, demons, and Satan. Demonic obsession is recognized by an uncontrollable and unusual preoccupation with demons, Satan, and the occult. A person may dabble in occult practices, constantly credit everything to Satan or demons, or be preoccupied with the study of demons and Satan.

A true Christian cannot be demon possessed. He may be obsessed with demons or oppressed by them, but a true believer cannot be possessed by a demon because the Holy Spirit cannot inhabit the same temple as an evil spirit (1 Corinthians 6:19-20). When you belong to God and are filled with the Holy Spirit, you cannot belong to Satan and be filled with his spirits at the same time. The Holy Ghost will not abide in the same "temple" with Satan.

Demons gain control in varied ways.

-Through generations: Demonic powers operating in parents and the sins of the parents can affect the next generation. This may account for demon possession or oppression of children such as recorded in Mark 7:24-30 and 9:17-21

-Through the mind: If Satan controls your thoughts, he will eventually control your actions. Lack of mental control eventually results in lack of use of the will. This leads to sinful actions. Continuing in sinful thoughts and actions can lead from oppression to possession and eventually to a reprobate mind such as is described in Romans 1--a mind totally controlled by evil thoughts. Demons also gain access through mind-altering drugs which reduce the ability to resist demons and grant increasing access to the mind. "Brain washing" and "mind control" also provide entrance points for the enemy into your mind.

-Through sinful actions: Sinful thoughts lead to sinful actions. For example, the thought of adultery is fulfilled in the actual act of adultery. Sin is rebellion, and rebellious thoughts and actions provides an entry point for demonic activity. When a believer continues in sinful thoughts or actions they "give place" to the Devil (Ephesians 4:27). Sins of involvement with the occult, including objects, literature, séances, etc., are actions which are especially dangerous and attract demonic powers.

-Through desire: Some people ask Satan for demonic power to enable them to perform supernatural acts. Others worship Satan or join Satanic cults.

-Through an empty house: Demons consider the body of the person they inhabit as their own house (Matthew 12:44). When a person who is delivered from demonic powers does not fill his spiritual house by the new birth experience and the infilling of the Holy Spirit, reentry may occur.

-Through permission: Sometimes God grants permission for demonic powers to operate through a trial--as in the case of Job--or judgment for sin--as in the example of King Saul.

Jesus dealt with demons. The teaching and ministry of Jesus demonstrated that demonic spirits are real forces of evil. Jesus accepted the fact that Satan is the ruler of a host of demons. He taught of the reality and power of demons. He said that casting out demons was one of the signs that the Kingdom of God had come. Read Matthew 12:22-30, Mark 3:22-27, and Luke 11:14-23 for a summary of what Jesus taught concerning demons. Jesus ministered deliverance to all who came with demonic problems (Acts 10:38).

You do not need to be afraid of demons. Jesus gives true believers power over all of the power of the enemy (Luke 10:19).

Jesus commissioned His followers to cast out demons. You are not to focus your ministry on casting out demons, but as you go into the world preaching the Gospel you will encounter demons that would hinder your ministry. You have the power and authority delegated by Jesus you to cast them out of yourself and others (Matthew 10:1,8; Mark 6:7; Mark 16:17; John 14:2).

DEALING WITH DEMONS AND DELIVERANCE:

Pray for discernment. Ask God to reveal the cause of the demonic influence. Ask for discernment in knowing how to minister and/or receive deliverance.

Faith, fasting, and prayer are essential when dealing with demons. Read the account in Matthew 17:14-21. Tools for deliverance include the Word of God (Ephesians 5:17; Hebrews 4:12); the blood of Jesus (Revelation 12:11); and the infilling power of the Holy Spirit (Acts 1:8; 2:38).

Determine the specific problem. The problem may be in the:

-Spiritual realm: Problems related to sin. These require a ministry of spiritual healing (repentance and forgiveness of sin).

-Physical realm: Bodily sickness caused by demonic spirits of infirmity.

-Emotional realm: Problems of anxiety, fear, anger, bitterness, resentment, guilt, doubt, failure, jealousy, selfishness, confusion, frustration, perfectionism in the energy of the flesh, unforgiveness, past situations.

-Mental realm: Problems stemming from negative thinking and attacks of Satan on the mind.

Remember: Because man is a triune being, problems in one realm affect the whole person so deal with the whole person, not just one area. Man is body, soul, spirit. Wholeness implies dealing with all of these.

Pray a prayer of deliverance. Focus on the specific problem--possession, obsession, oppression, etc. You do not have to persuade God to deliver by your prayer. Just as salvation is readily available, the same is true of deliverance. Just as salvation is based on the condition of faith, so is deliverance. God wants to deliver, just as He wants to save.   Here is a prayer of deliverance to pray over yourself or to someone to whom you may be ministering:

"In the name of Jesus Christ and based on the authority of His power, His Word, His blood, and His Holy Spirit..."

...This establishes the power base for deliverance...

"...I bind you...."
*...**Jesus taught to bind the strong man first before attempting to cast him out...***
"...and I command you..."

*...**Ministering deliverance is a prayer of authority, not of retreat. You can speak quietly, but you must take authority over the forces of evil in the name of Jesus. Look directly into the eyes of the person as you speak.***

"...the spirit of_________" or "...you foul spirit of Satan..."

*...**if the spirit has been identified either through spiritual or natural discernment, then name it specifically; otherwise, generally.***

"...to depart...."

*...**this is the casting out process...***

"...without harming________(your name or the name of the person being delivered), or anyone in this house, and without creating noise or disturbance"

*...**Sometimes the demon will try to harm the person or create a disturbance.***

"I forbid you to reenter..."

*...**Remember that Jesus used this command...***

"...and I lose the Holy Spirit to cleanse and fill this vessel through the power delegated by Jesus Christ...

*...**We are told to lose as well as bind. If you have identified a specific spirit, name it.***

", in the name of Jesus Christ."

Recognize the signs of deliverance. In cases of demonic possession, sometimes demons come out with a struggle, such as crying out or throwing the person on the floor. When demons have departed and their hold has been broken, there will be a sense of release and joy, like the lifting of a weight.

Take follow-up steps. Jesus emphasized the importance of follow-up so that demons will not return (Matthew 12:43-45).

-Pray a prayer of renouncing. After deliverance, pray a prayer of confession, repentance, and renouncing of any sins or involvements connected with the demonic.

-Destroy occult items. These would include idols, voodoo items, witchcraft equipment, books, charms, etc.

-Fill the spiritual void. When a demon is cast out, he will seek another body through which to operate. A demon is restless and discontent outside of a human body. It is only by indwelling and controlling a human life that a demon is able to fulfill Satan's evil purposes. Because of the danger of a demon returning to his former victim accompanied by worse spirits, the spiritual void must be filled. A person must receive Jesus Christ as Savior and be filled with the Holy Spirit. (Acts 2:38-39) He should continually immerse himself in prayer and the Word of God and become part of a community of believers.

-Testify of the deliverance. Jesus told the demoniac of Gadarene to tell others about his deliverance (Mark 5:19-20). Revelation 12:11 confirms that we overcome the powers of Satan by the word of our testimony.

Protect yourself from demonic powers. Here are specific ways to protect yourself from demonic powers:

-Accept Jesus Christ as Savior. (Acts 2:38-39)

-Avoid sin. After you are saved, keep yourself from sin, for through sin you "give place to the devil" or provide opportunity for him to oppress you.

-Be filled with the Holy Spirit. Demonic spirits and the Spirit of God cannot inhabit the same spiritual vessel.

-Avoid an obsessive interest in demons. It is not wrong to study what God's Word says about them or expositions based on God's Word, but do not read secular books, attend séances, etc., to learn more about demons.

-Avoid any contact with the occult. Do not consult witches, shaman, astrologers, horoscopes, or card, palm, or tea leaf readers. Do not serve false gods or allow idols to come into your home (Deuteronomy 7:25-26).

WHAT GOD'S WORD SAYS ABOUT DEMONS AND DELIVERANCE:

Do not turn to mediums or seek out spiritualist, for you will be defiled by them. I am the Lord your God. (Leviticus 19:31)

When you enter the land the Lord your God is giving you, do not learn to imitate the detestable ways of the nations there. Let no one be found among you who sacrifices his son or daughter in the fire, who practices divination or sorcery, interprets omens, engages in witchcraft, or casts spells, or who is a medium or spiritualist or who consults the dead. Anyone who does these things is detestable to the Lord, (Deuteronomy 18:9-12)

My enemies turn back; they stumble and perish before you. (Psalm 9:3)

For in the day of trouble he will keep me safe in his dwelling; he will hide me in the shelter of his tabernacle and set me high upon a rock. Then my head will be exalted above the enemies who surround me; at his tabernacle will I sacrifice with shouts of joy; I will sing and make music to the Lord. (Psalm 27:5-6)

The Lord is my strength and my shield; my heart trusts in him, and I am helped. My heart leaps for joy and I will give thanks to him in song. (Psalm 28:7)

This poor man called, and the Lord heard him; he saved him out of all his troubles. The angel of the Lord encamps around those who fear him, and he delivers them. (Psalm 34:6-7)

The righteous cry out, and the Lord hears them; he delivers them from all their troubles. (Psalm 34:17)

A righteous man may have many troubles, but the Lord delivers him from them all. (Psalm 34:19)

Read Psalm 91.

News about him spread all over Syria, and people brought to him all who were ill with various diseases, those suffering severe pain, the demon-possessed, those having seizures, and the paralyzed, and he healed them. (Matthew 4:24)

When evening came, many who were demon-possessed were brought to him, and he drove out the spirits with a word and healed all the sick... (Matthew 8:16)

He called his twelve disciples to him and gave them authority to drive out evil spirits and to heal every disease and sickness. (Matthew 10:1)

If Satan drives out Satan, he is divided against himself. How then can his kingdom stand? And if I drive out demons by Beelzebub, by whom do your people drive them out? So then, they will be your judges. But if I drive out demons by the Spirit of God, then the kingdom of God has come upon you. "Or again, how can anyone enter a strong man's house and carry off his possessions unless he first ties up the strong man? Then he can rob his house. (Matthew 12:26-29)

Whenever the evil spirits saw him, they fell down before him and cried out, "You are the Son of God." (Mark 3:11)

And these signs will accompany those who believe: In my Name, they will drive out demons; they will speak in new tongues; they will pick up snakes with their hands; and when they drink deadly poison, it will not hurt them at all; they will place their hands on sick people, and they will get well." (Mark 16:17-18)

In the synagogue there was a man possessed by a demon, an evil spirit. He cried out at the top of his voice, "Ha! What do you want with us, Jesus of Nazareth? Have you come to destroy us? I know who you are--the Holy One of God!" "Be quiet!" Jesus said sternly. "Come out of him!" Then the demon threw the man down before them all and came out without injuring him. All the people were amazed and said to each other, "What is this teaching? With authority and power, he gives orders to evil spirits and they come out!" (Luke 4:33-36)

When the sun was setting, the people brought to Jesus all who had various kinds of sickness, and laying his hands on each one, he healed them. Moreover, demons came out of many people, shouting, "You are the Son of God!" But he rebuked them and would not allow them to speak, because they knew he was the Christ. (Luke 4:40-41)

He replied, "I saw Satan fall like lightning from heaven. I have given you authority to trample on snakes and scorpions and to overcome all the power of the enemy; nothing will harm you." (Luke 10:18-19)

The thief comes only to steal and kill and destroy; I have come that they may have life, and have it to the full. (John 10:10)

I tell you the truth, anyone who has faith in me will do what I have been doing. He will do even greater things than these, because I am going to the Father. (John 14:12)

Crowds gathered also from the towns around Jerusalem, bringing their sick and those tormented by evil spirits, and all of them were healed. (Acts 5:16)

With shrieks, evil spirits came out of many, and many paralytics and cripples were healed. (Acts 8:7)

You know what has happened throughout Judea, beginning in Galilee after the baptism that John preached--how God anointed Jesus of Nazareth with the Holy Spirit and power, and how he went around doing good and healing all who were under the power of the devil, because God was with him. (Acts 10:37-38)

You, however, are controlled not by the sinful nature but by the Spirit, if the Spirit of God lives in you. And if anyone does not have the Spirit of Christ, he does not belong to Christ. But if Christ is in you, your body is dead because of sin, yet your spirit is alive because of righteousness. And if the Spirit of him who raised Jesus from the dead is living in you, he who raised Christ from the dead will also give life to your mortal bodies through his Spirit, who lives in you. (Romans 8:9-11)

No, but the sacrifices of pagans are offered to demons, not to God, and I do not want you to be participants with demons. You cannot drink the cup of the Lord and the cup of demons too; you cannot have a part in both the Lord's table and the table of demons. (1 Corinthians 10:20-21)

Put on the full armor of God so that you can take your stand against the devil's schemes. For our struggle is not against flesh and blood, but against the rulers, against the authorities, against the powers of this dark world and against the spiritual forces of evil in the heavenly realms. Therefore, put on the full armor of God, so that when the day of evil comes, you may be able to stand your ground, and after you have done everything, to stand. Stand firm then, with the belt of truth buckled around your waist, with the breastplate of righteousness in place, and with your feet fitted with the readiness that comes from the gospel of peace. In addition to all this, take up the shield of faith, with which you can extinguish all the flaming arrows of the evil one. Take the helmet of salvation and the sword of the Spirit, which is the word of God. And pray in the Spirit on all occasions with all kinds of prayers and requests. With this in mind, be alert and always keep on praying for all the saints. (Ephesians 6:11-18)

The Spirit clearly says that in later times some will abandon the faith and follow deceiving spirits and things taught by demons. Such teachings come through hypocritical liars, whose consciences have been seared as with a hot iron. (1 Timothy 4:1-2)

The Lord will rescue me from every evil attack and will bring me safely to his heavenly kingdom. To him be glory for ever and ever. Amen. (2 Timothy 4:18)

Submit yourselves, then, to God. Resist the devil, and he will flee from you. (James 4:7)

For if God did not spare angels when they sinned, but sent them to hell, putting them into gloomy dungeons to be held for judgment; if he did not spare the ancient world when he brought the flood on its ungodly people, but protected Noah, a preacher of righteousness, and seven others; if he condemned the cities of Sodom and Gomorrah by burning them to ashes, and made them an example of what is going to happen to the ungodly; and if he rescued Lot, a righteous man, who was distressed by the filthy lives of lawless men (for that righteous man, living among them day after day, was tormented in his righteous soul by the lawless deeds he saw and heard)-- if this is so, then the Lord knows how to rescue godly men from trials and to hold the unrighteous for the day of judgment, while continuing their punishment. (2 Peter 2:4-9)

He who does what is sinful is of the devil, because the devil has been sinning from the beginning. The reason the Son of God appeared was to destroy the devil's work.
(1 John 3:8)

Dear friends, do not believe every spirit, but test the spirits to see whether they are from God, because many false prophets have gone out into the world. This is how you can recognize the Spirit of God: Every spirit that acknowledges that Jesus Christ has come in the flesh is from God, but every spirit that does not acknowledge Jesus is not from God. This is the spirit of the antichrist, which you have heard is coming and even now is already in the world. You, dear children, are from God and have overcome them, because the one who is in you is greater than the one who is in the world. They are from the world and therefore speak from the viewpoint of the world, and the world listens to them. We are from God, and whoever knows God listens to us; but whoever is not from God does not listen to us. This is how we recognize the Spirit of truth and the spirit of falsehood. (1 John 4:1-6)

And the angels who did not keep their positions of authority but abandoned their own home-- these he has kept in darkness, bound with everlasting chains for judgment on the great Day. (Jude 1:6)

And there was war in heaven. Michael and his angels fought against the dragon, and the dragon and his angels fought back. But he was not strong enough, and they lost their place in heaven. The great dragon was hurled down--that ancient serpent called the devil, or Satan, who leads the whole world astray. He was hurled to the earth, and his angels with him. (Revelation 12:7-9)

And the devil, who deceived them, was thrown into the lake of burning sulfur, where the beast and the false prophet had been thrown. They will be tormented day and night for ever and ever. (Revelation 20:10)

CONCLUSION

How to Get Rid of "it" though Personal Deliverance

When you understand self-deliverance, you will keep yourself from being bond; you will keep yourself healthy, physically and spiritually and be free from spiritual pollution. Every day, you will enjoy divine health and will not be spending your money on drugs and hospital bills.

Sometimes, there may not be a minister who is anointed and knowledgeable about deliverance to help you. Sometimes, you can be heavily attacked and the next service is about four days away. What do you do? You should never allow evil spirits to reside in your life. If you lack adequate time to do a self-deliverance in the mornings, after your quiet time, then, when you're having your bath, you could do it.

Whatever the causes of our spiritual afflictions, there are several proven steps we may try to help ourselves find freedom and healing. If these steps do not resolve your situation, then perhaps it is time to ask for help:

Step 1 — Conversion

Deliverance from any level of bondage, or harassment (collectively called, "spiritual afflictions") cannot be achieved without personal conversion. Deliverance from milder forms of spiritual affliction may often be achieved by the various acts of personal conversion—Acts of Contrition, Faith, Hope, Charity, and Consecration. "Prayer Acts" and other prayers, with fasting, and various devotions are often effective to drive evil spirits away:

So humble yourselves before God. Resist the Devil, and he will flee from you. Draw close to God, and God will draw close to you. — (James 4:7,8)

The first step, therefore, is make up your mind to live the Christ-life; or if already doing so, to persevere in living the Christ-life. This internal conversion, which is a conscious decision and determination to follow Christ and all of His teachings, precedes all other steps to deliverance. Without conversion to the Faith in Jesus Christ and participation in His family, the Church, deliverance, even if seemingly effective for a while, cannot be successful in the long run. It is the *"Truth"* that makes us free (John 8:31b), not prayers, rituals, counseling, or personal will in themselves. It is the confrontation with Truth that sends the demons running back to hell. This is why the method of Deliverance Counseling we use is called a *"Truth Encounter"*. As demons are confronted with the Truth, and as we are confronted with the Truth, of whom we are in Christ, we gain freedom. The foundation of all truth is Jesus Christ, who is Truth (John 14:6). Without our Lord Jesus Christ, we can never know truth or obtain it.

Some people believe they are unable to make a profession of faith in Jesus Christ. In such cases the person should ask God for help—ask Him for the faith that will save, deliver, and heal.

If we are willing to accept the gift of faith from God, our Lord will give it to us when we ask:

67

And I tell you, Ask, and it will be given you; seek, and you will find; knock, and it will be opened to you. For every one who asks receives, and he who seeks finds, and to him who knocks it will be opened. What father among you, if his son asks for a fish, will instead of a fish give him a serpent; or if he asks for an egg, will give him a scorpion? If you then, who are evil, know how to give good gifts to your children, how much more will the heavenly Father give the Holy Spirit to those who ask him! — (Luke 11:9-13)

Sincerely ask God for the faith that brings saving faith, the faith of conversion to the One, that is Jesus Christ, whom who declares:

I am the way, and the truth, and the life; no one comes to the Father, but by me (John 14:6) .... Come to me, all who labor and are heavy laden, and I will give you rest (Matthew 11:28) .... I will not reject anyone who comes to me (John 6:37) .... [rather] take my yoke upon you, and learn from me; for I am gentle and lowly in heart, and you will find rest for your souls. For my yoke is easy, and my burden is light (Matt 11:29-30)

Step 2 — Repentance

Essential to growing closer to God in faith, devotion, and love is to repent of those behaviors, desires, beliefs, and ideas that are sinful. The definition of sin is much broader than most people imagine. A definition of sin:

Sin is an offense against reason, truth, and right conscience; it is a failure in genuine love for God and neighbor caused by a perverse attachment to certain goods. Its wounds the nature of man and injures human solidarity. It has been defined as "an utterance, a deed, or a desire contrary to the eternal law."

Sin is an offense against God: *"Against you, you alone, have I sinned, and done that which is evil in your sight"* (Ps 51:4). Sin sets itself against God's love for us and turns our hearts away from it. Like the first sin (of Adam and Eve), it is disobedience, a revolt against God through the will to become "like gods" (Gen 3:5), knowing and determining good and evil. Sin is thus "love of oneself even to contempt of God." In this proud self-exaltation, sin is diametrically opposed to the obedience of Jesus, which achieves our salvation (cf. Phil 2:6-9).

We must repent of our sin, but repentance involves more than merely "turning away" from sin. Repentance must also renounce all that opposes God and all that He finds sinful. This includes renouncing Satan and his ways, renouncing personal sins, and renouncing all that leads us to sin. Some of the common sins and situations that interfere with deliverance include: involvement in non-Christian activities like the occult; persistent situational sins such as living together without marriage or remarriage without annulment of previous marriages; maintaining improper or problematic friendships; illegal activities of any sort; and sins that have become habitual such as pornography, masturbation, fornication, gossip, lying, stealing, etc.

The three greatest stumbling blocks to deliverance is Pride, Rebellion, and Unforgiveness and all the things that go along with those three sins. Repentance of Pride, Rebellion, and Unforgiveness is required to even hope for deliverance. Repentance also includes the firm amendment to avoid sin, and the near occasion of sin, in the future. Repentance requires a *complete* turnaround of our lives, a becoming a *"new man"*, so that...

...you should put away the old self of your former way of life, corrupted through deceitful desires, and be renewed in the spirit of your minds, and put on the new self, created in God's way in righteousness and holiness of truth. Therefore, putting away falsehood, speak the truth, each one to his neighbor, for we are members one of another...(thus) do not leave room for the devil (Eph 4:22-25,26b)

Step 3 — Confession

With faith and contrition of heart, repentance of mind, firm purpose to avoid sin and that which leads us to sin, we must now confess our sins before our God who is a God of forgiveness and mercy. This is a critical step that we will discuss at length.

The manner of our confession differs, but within our respective traditions, confession is required:

If we confess our sins, he is faithful and just, and will forgive our sins and cleanse us from all unrighteousness. (1 John 1:9)

... if you confess with your mouth that Jesus is Lord and believe in your heart that God raised him from the dead, you will be saved. For one believes with the heart and so is justified, and one confesses with the mouth and so is saved. (Romans 10:9-10)

"Confess your sins to each other and pray for each other so that you may be healed. The earnest prayer of a righteous person has great power and wonderful results" (James 5:16).

This confidant maybe one's pastor or another minister, or a trusted friend. We must be careful when choosing an "accountability partner." Since we will be revealing very private and sensitive information about ourselves, it is critically important to trust whoever we choose as a confidant to be discreet and to keep absolutely confidential the information we tell them.

There is wisdom in presenting oneself to an "accountability partner." Personal accountability is upheld when we confess to another person whom may hold us accountable for our actions. Confessing our sins to one another is a powerful way to break the bonds of sin in our lives. It is much harder to confess our sins to one another than to simply say, *"Lord, forgive me"*. While God is forgiving, of course, it is the demands of personal accountability before another human being that brings our confession into grounded reality that strengthens our commitment to turn away from sin in the future.

Religious ministers, psychologists, counselors, and others including the Deliverance Counselors of agency, are also bound either by law, ethical codes, or contract with the client (or bound by any combination thereof) to keep private and confidential all that is revealed to them. In addition, those in the ministerial and helping professions are usually trained in the ethics, legalities, and culture of maintaining confidentiality. They are use to keeping private the personal information of their patients and clients. Friends, on the other hand, may not have such training and may not be use to the culture of confidentiality. Thus, if one's confidant is not a pastor, or at least a minister, psychologist, or counselor bound by law and/or ethical codes, take care to ensure the chosen confidant understands thoroughly that he must keep private all that he hears and may not discuss it with anyone, not even with his spouse.

There is a great psychological comfort in hearing the words, "I forgive you" or the equivalent, "I absolve you of your sins." Our Father in heaven understands this psychological need. Thus, in His great love for us, He provided a way for us to hear those words in His name. It is God who ultimately forgives sins, but God, according to His sovereign authority chose to delegate this authority to His validly ordained priests. This power was given to the Apostles in John 20:22-23 and was passed on from them to those whom they appointed.

Our Father in heaven also knows and understands our need to be a family and for the family to come to our aid when we are hurting, to offer forgiveness when we fall, and to provide healing and strength to help us grow in faith. God forgives you when you appeal to Him with your heart-felt and sincere repentance and confession. Follow the tradition of your denomination and always offer a prayer for forgiveness as soon as possible after sinning. Then, in obedience to the Bible, seek accountability by confession to a confidant to complete your healing.

Step 4 — Removing the Greatest Stumbling blocks: Pride, Rebellion, and Forgiveness

We have already mentioned that the three biggest stumbling blocks to deliverance is usually Pride, Rebellion, and Unforgiveness. These three sins distance us from God. To draw closer to God we need to give up our pride, obey our Lord's teachings, and forgive those who hurt us.

In Deliverance Counseling we help our clients through exercises to locate pockets of pride and rebellion and to rid themselves of these sins with the help of God through prayer. Forgiveness, however, tends to be the most difficult, partly because of pride or even rebellion perhaps, but mostly because of deeply emotional issues surrounding the circumstances of the hurts someone has given us. Whatever the causes of our unforgiveness, deliverance is not possible until we can come to forgive, thus we shall discuss this topic at some length too.

The following guide is rather long, but this step is one of the most important. One simple MUST deals with Pride, Rebellion, and Unforgiveness if deliverance and healing is to be permanently possible.

Pride: Pride is the essential sin that leads to most other sins. It is the sin of Lucifer that led him to rebel against God resulting in his expulsion from heaven and becoming Satan.

Pride is a killer. Pride says, "I can do it! I can get myself out of this mess without God and without anyone else's helped." No, we can't! We absolutely need God, and we desperately need each other.

Pride also says "I know the best and most efficient way and how dare others get in the way of that" or "How dare things not go my way" or "How dare some person or something get in the way of what I want to do." Impatience is a factor of pride. Other ways impatience reveals our pride is getting impatient when we cannot find our car keys, or when we are late to a meeting, or if someone is driving too slowly for us on the hi-way, or when the computer acts up and interrupts our train of thought.

Impatience is the sister to Pride because it is caused essentially by our desire to have things our own way, in our own time, and according to our own preferences.

Pride is also the engine behind egotism (thinking more of oneself than one ought) and behind false humility (putting oneself down to be less than what one actually is). Pride is the force behind resistance to lawful and appropriate authority — whether that authority is a parent, teacher, police officer, government, employer, or the Church.

Pride is the basis of thinking of oneself as better than others, being pompous, and having contempt toward one's neighbors, employers, other family members, or the Church and her ministers.

Pride can also rear its ugly head in more subtle ways such as reluctance to apologize when we need to apologize, demanding our rights merely because it is our right, being inappropriately unkind or rude, jealousy, being quick-tempered, moodiness, brooding over wrongs done by others to oneself, depression and despair, or demanding that we are right about something, when indeed we are right about the issue, even though the issue is unimportant or can be handled differently (this is a major phenomenon in marriages, families, and friendships — the phrase "We need to choose our battles" is an important remedy for this).

Other ways that Pride expresses itself include: by taking personal credit for gifts or possessions and thus refusing to acknowledge that we have what we have by God's Providence; glorying in our achievements as if they were not primary a result of God's grace and divine goodness; by minimizing one's defeats; by claiming qualities that are not actually possessed; magnifying the faults and defects of others or dwelling upon the defects and faults of others.

James 4:6-10 and 1 Peter 5:1-10 reveals that spiritual conflict follows pride.

Examine yourself for these and any other attributes of pride and then pray:

Dear Heavenly Father. You have said that pride goes before destruction and an arrogant spirit before stumbling (Prov. 16:18). I confess that I have not denied myself, picked up my cross daily, and followed You (Matt. 16:24). In so doing I have given ground to the enemy in my life. I have believed that I could be successful and live victoriously by my own strength and resources. I now confess that I have sinned against You by placing my will before You and by centering my life around self instead of You.

I now renounce the self-life and by so doing cancel all the ground that has been gained in my life by the enemies of the Lord Jesus Christ. I pray that You will guide me so that I will do nothing from selfishness or empty conceit, but with humility of mind that I will regard others as more important than myself (Phil. 2:3). Enable me through love to serve others and in honor prefer others (Rom. 12:10). Amen.

Rebellion: We often place our confidence in the flesh not only with the "I can do it myself" attitude but each time we assert our own opinions above the teachings of Christ. It is a pride and a rebellion to say, "I want to do it my way" or "I want to think the way I want" without regard to the ways God teaches us to go and to believe. This is an arrogance that not only can get us into major trouble but also forms a major vulnerability for demons to come into our life.

Rebelling against God and His authority gives Satan an opportunity to attack. As our commanding general, the Lord Jesus Christ says, *"Get into ranks and follow Me. I will not lead you into temptation, but I will deliver you from evil."*

The Bible teaches us that it is the will of God for us to be obedient to parents, to civil government, to the Church, and to the pastors who are over us. We have two biblical responsibilities in regard to these authority figures: 1) Pray for them; and 2) submit to them. The only time God permits us to disobey those in authority over us is when they require of us an act or acquiescence in ways that are contrary to Church Law, Natural Law, or Divine Law.

Being under authority is an act of faith; we are trusting God to work through His established lines of authority. The authority that God has ordained does not mean, however, that we are to submit to abuse from those authorities. In those cases where someone in authority over us is abusing us in any way, then we need to act in appropriate ways according to the situation — such as appeal to the state for protection and relief for civil or criminal issues; or appeal to Church authorities on some issue involving religion or our parish; or make appropriate decisions such as terminating an abusive relationship, etc. Whoever the authority, who is abusing, we need to pray for the offender and to forgive him; but we are not required to be a doormat or target of their abuse.

Some of the lines of authority mentioned in the Bible include:

- Church leaders (Hebrews 13:17; Matthew 18:15-18)
- Parents (Ephesians 6: 1-3; Exodus 20:12)
- Husbands (1 Peter 3:1-3; Ephesians 5:23-24)
- Employers (1 Peter 2:18-21)
- Civil Government (Romans 13:1-5; 1 Timothy 2:1-3; 1 Peter 2:13-16)

Examine yourself for any areas of rebellion (deliberate driving faster than the speed limit is rebellion, too, you know!) and then pray:

Dear Heavenly Father. You have said that rebellion is as the sin of witchcraft and insubordination is as iniquity and idolatry (1 Sam. 15.23). I know that in action and attitude I have sinned against You with a rebellious heart. I ask Your forgiveness for my rebellion and pray that by the shed blood of the Lord Jesus Christ, strengthened by intercession of the that all ground gained by evil spirits because of my rebelliousness be canceled and taken back. I pray that You will shed light on all my ways that I may know the full extent of my rebelliousness, and I now choose to adopt a submissive spirit and a servant's heart. Amen.

Unforgiveness: Jesus Himself discusses the seriousness of failing to forgive. He tells us that failure to forgive those who hurt us will result in our not being forgiven ourselves by God. *"Forgive us our trespasses (sins) as we forgive those who trespass (sin) against us"*. The *Our Father*, the Lord's Prayer, which most all of us know and pray, Jesus teaches us that God will be as forgiving to us as we are to others.

Indeed, how can we expect God to forgive us when we do not forgive our brothers? Consider the follow teachings from Holy Scripture:

If you forgive those who sin against you, your heavenly Father will forgive you. But if you refuse to forgive others, your Father will not forgive your sins (Matthew 6:14,15).

But when you are praying, first forgive anyone you are holding a grudge against, so that your Father in heaven will forgive your sins, too (Mark 11:25).

If you forgive others, you will be forgiven. (Luke 6:37b)

Forgiveness is not about emotions and feelings. You can still be hurting, angry and upset and still decide to forgive. Forgiveness involves a mental decision, a decision of will, an act of your free will, even though you may not "Feel it".

The true nature of forgiveness:

1. **Forgiveness is not forgetting:** People who try to forget find that cannot. It is an unfortunate quirk of the English language with the phrase, "Forgive and forget". In actuality this phrase does not mean to "forget" in the sense of not remembering what happened; of course, we will remember. God says He will "remember our sins no more" (Heb. 10: 17), but God, being omniscient, obviously cannot literally forget. "Remember no more" means that God will never use the past against us (Ps. 103:12).

   To forget is really "to let go". We need to *"let go and let God"*. We let go of the past, but more importantly we let go of the hurt. As long as we do not forgive, as long as we do not let go, we allow the offender of our wounds continue to hurt us.
2. **Forgiveness is a choice not a feeling:** Since God requires us to forgive, <u>it is something we can do</u>. God will NEVER ask us to do something that is impossible for us to do; that would be cruel and God is a loving God.

   Forgiveness, however, is difficult for us because it pulls against our feelings and emotional hurts. Forgiveness is not about forgetting our feelings or our emotional hurts. We often will not "feel" like forgiving, but we must forgive anyway. As the Lord Prayer teaches us, God forgives us "as we forgive others". But how can God require this of us when we have been hurt so badly?

   God does not expect your feelings and emotional hurts to be healed overnight. He knows and understands our feelings and our hurts. He is a compassionate God and will help us to heal over time, as we are able. What God expects of us is not an immediate emotional healing, but a decision of will to forgive, a decision of will to trust Him to take care of the offender and to heal us, a decision of will to ask God for, and to commit to, being healed of our wounds.

3. **Forgiveness is not letting the person off the hook:** Forgiving is about you letting go, but it is not letting the offender off the hook. He will still pay for what he did, either before the Law or before God or both.

Forgiving is surely difficult for us because it pulls against our concept of justice. We want revenge for offenses suffered. But we are told never to take our own revenge (Rom. 12:9). Revenge does more damage to us than it punishes the offender. God's justice will prevail, no one can escape it. Never fear, those who hurt us will be held accountable, but we must let God deal with it. In order for God to deal with it, we need to let Him deal with it by letting go.

"Why should I let them off the hook?" But doing that is precisely the problem — we are still hooked to them, still bound by our past when we do not forgive.

To forgive does not mean letting the person off the hook; it means letting yourself off the hook.

4. **But you don't understand how much this person hurt me:** The problem is that when we do not forgive we, in essence, allow the person to still hurt us! The question is, "How do we stop the pain?" The answer is **to forgive!**

It is important to understand that we do not forgive someone for their sake; we do it for our sake so we can be free. Our need to forgive is not an issue between the offender and us; it is between us and God.

5. **Forgiveness is agreeing to live with the consequences of another's sin:** Forgiveness is costly. We pay the price of the evil we forgive. We are going to live with those consequences whether we want to or not; our only choice is whether or not we will do so in the slavery of bitterness and unforgiveness or with the freedom of forgiveness.

Jesus took the consequences of our sin upon Himself. All true forgiveness is substitution because no one really forgives without bearing the consequences of the other person's sin. God the Father *"made Him who knew no sin to be sin on our behalf, that we might become the righteousness of God in Him"* (2 Cor. 5:2 1).

Where is the justice? We might ask. It is the Cross that makes forgiveness legally and morally right: *"For the death that He died, He died to sin, once for all"* (Rom. 6: 10). This doesn't mean that we tolerate sin. We must always stand against sin, but we must give the offender to God and get on with our life.

6. **How do we forgive from our heart?** First, we acknowledge the hurt and the hate. If our forgiveness does not visit the emotional core of our life, it will be incomplete. Many feel the pain of interpersonal offenses, but they will not

acknowledge it. Let God bring the pain to the surface so He can deal with it. This is where the healing takes place.

Do not wait to forgive until we feel like forgiving; we will never get there. Feelings take time to heal mostly <u>after</u> the choice to forgive is made and Satan has lost his place (Eph. 4:26, 27). Freedom is what will be gained, not a feeling.

7. **Summary of Points on Forgiveness:**
   o Forgiveness is necessary to have fellowship with God.
   o It is not forgetting.
   o It is a choice.
   o Letting the offender off <u>our</u> hook is what frees us.
   o The offender is not off God's hook.
   o God says, "Revenge is mine."
   o You must acknowledge the hurt and the hate.
   o Forgiveness means we are agreeing to live with the consequences of another's sin — which we have to do anyway.
   o The justice is in the cross.
   o Choice is between the slavery of bitterness or the freedom of forgiveness.
   o Forgiveness means not using the past against the offender.
   o Forgiveness <u>does not</u> mean tolerating the sin or abuse.
   o Why forgive? To stop the pain! As we live in unforgiveness the offender still hurts us!
   o The issue of forgiveness is between you and God only.
   o The act of forgiveness is for your sake, and for your freedom.

Think about the people in your life for whom you need to forgive, people to whom you hold bitterness, people who have hurt you or disappointed you in anyway, or for whom you hold any kind of grudge. Be sure to ALWAYS include your parents, siblings, spouse, and YOURSELF. There is always something to forgive in our families and in ourselves.

Record all the names you can think of on a sheet of paper and a brief note as to why you need to forgive them. If you do not remember names, list them by what you do remember, such as "the guy in sixth grade with the red hat". If you cannot remember why you need to forgive someone on your list that is okay; forgive them for whatever it was — God knows.

After preparing this list ask God to bring to your mind anyone you have forgotten. It is not unusual to forget, or to push aside from our conscious mind, incidents and even the names of people whom have hurt us. These hidden hurts and wounds need to be healed as well. Thus, ask God to bring to your mind any person you have forgotten for whom you need to forgive, for whom you hold a grudge against, for which you are bitter, for those who have hurt you, with the following prayer:

Father in heaven, please bring to my mind the names of any people for whom I have held bitterness towards, grudges against, or have not forgiven for the hurts they have caused me. Help me to remember all these hurts so that they may be offered to You, O Lord, and healed from my soul so that I may live the truly victorious Christ-life. Amen.

Add to your list the names of anyone God may bring to your mind.

Now it is time to pray...

The following prayer needs to be said for each person on the list for which you need to forgive. Do not go to the next person on the list until you are sure you have dealt with all the remembered pain.

As you pray, God may bring to your mind various offending people and experiences that has been totally forgotten. Allow God to do this even if it is painful. Remember this process of forgiveness is for your sake because God wants you to be free.

Remember also that by forgiving the offender we are not rationalizing or trying to explain the offender's behavior. Forgiveness deals with the victim's pain, your pain, not another's excuses. Positive feelings will follow in time; freeing you from the past is the critical issue now.

If you are willing to forgive for your sake, so that you can walk away from this webpage free in Christ, free from the past and from person who hurt you, pray the introductory prayer below and then pray the "Prayer to Forgive" for each person on your list:

Heavenly Father, I now ask for your help in forgiving all those people on my list. Although I am still hurt and angry with them, I know that they are your children and that you love them more than I can possibly know. For this reason, my God, I ask you to help me forgive them. I lay down all bitterness, resentment and hatred for this person and I freely choose to forgive them. Teach me to be more merciful, my God, and help me be always willing, just as you are always willing, to forgive those who sin against me. Amen."

Prayer to Forgive

Lord, I forgive ___________________________________ for (specifically identify all offenses and painful memories).

May God heal you and bless you!

Step 5 — Know Who You Are in Christ!

In order to gain freedom, it is important to know who you are in Christ. Thus, you need to evaluate the concept you have of yourself, to acknowledge the truth about God and about yourself; about your relationship and ideas about God and about the manner of our lives.

We often deceive ourselves about our position in Christ and our relationship with Him. For example, we may say to ourselves: "This isn't going to work" or "I wish I could believe this but I can't" or perhaps even more direct deceptions or denials concerning the promises of God for His children. Areas of deception that we may have include:

1. **Self-Deception** (telling ourselves things that are not true)

- o Listening to God's words but thinking we do not have to do it (Ja 1:22; 4:17)
- o Thinking we have no sin or do not sin (1 Jn 1:8)
- o Thinking that we are something when we are not (Gal 6:3)
- o Believing that we will not reap what we sow (Gal 6:7)
- o Thinking we are wise and sophisticated in the 21st century (1 Cor 3:18, 19)
- o Believing that the unrighteous will reach heaven (1 Cor 6:9)
- o Thinking we can associate with bad company and not be corrupted (1 Cor 15:33)

2. **Self-Defense** (defending ourselves instead of trusting Christ)
   - o Denial (conscious or subconscious)
   - o Fantasy (escape from the real world)
   - o Emotional insulation (withdraw to avoid rejection)
   - o Regression (reverting back to a less threatening time in the past)
   - o Displacement (taking out frustrations on others)
   - o Projection (blaming others or accusing others of things we ourselves have done)
   - o Rationalization (defending self though verbal excursion)

To counter these and other deceptions we tell ourselves we need to exercise faith. Faith is the response to Truth and believing the truth is a CHOICE (not a feeling). If we say, "I want to believe God, but I just can't," then we are deceiving ourselves. Of course, we can believe God. We know that God does not lie. Faith is something we DECIDE to do; it is not something we FEEL like doing. Believing the truth does not make it true; rather it is TRUE, therefore we believe it.

Examine yourself and how you may deceive yourself with "self-deceptions" and "Self-Defense" mechanisms. The pray the following prayer: ...

Prayer to Know the Truth:

Dear Heavenly Father. I know that You desire truth in the inner self and that facing this truth is the way of liberation (John 8:32). I acknowledge that I have been deceived by the father of lies (John 8:44) and that I have deceived myself (1 John 1:8). I pray in the name of the Lord Jesus Christ, and since by faith I have received You into my life and am now seated with Christ in the heavenliest (Eph 2:6), I ask you Father to command all deceiving spirits to depart from me. I now ask You to *"search me, O God, and know my heart: try me and know my anxious thoughts; and see if there be any hurtful way in me, and lead me in the everlasting way"* (Ps. 139:23, 24) In the name of Christ Jesus I pray. Amen.

Knowing the truth about oneself, overcoming self-deceptions and the mechanism of self-defense that hide who we really are, includes understanding our faith in Christ. It is by Christ that our lives have meaning and substance.

The following prayer is the substance of that faith:

Affirmations

I believe that I am a child of God (1 Jn. 3:1-3) and that I am seated with Christ in the heavenlies (Eph. 2:6). I believe that I was saved by the grace of God through faith that is a gift and not the result of my own efforts or merits (Eph 2:8).

I choose to be strong in the Lord and in the strength of His might (Eph 6:10). I put no confidence in the flesh (Phil 3:3) for the weapons of warfare are not of the flesh (2 Cor. 10:4). I put on the whole armor of God (Eph. 6:10-20), and I resolve to stand firm in my faith and to resist the evil one.

I believe that Jesus Christ has all authority in heaven and on earth (Matt 28:18) and that He is the head over all rule and authority (Col 2:10). I believe that Satan and his demons and wicked spirits are subject to the Lord Jesus Christ and therefore to me in Christ since I am a member of Christ's body (Eph 1:19-23).

I believe that apart from Christ I can do nothing (John 15:5) so I declare my dependence upon Him.

I choose to abide in Christ in order to bear much fruit and to glorify the Lord (Jn 15:8) and to accomplish the work of sanctification that Christ began in me through the Cross (James 2).

I believe that since I am a member go God's royal family I have the authority, in the name of Christ Jesus, to ask the Father to command the devil to leave my presence, as I obey the command to resist the devil (James 4:7).

I reject any counterfeit gifts or works of Satan and his minions in my life.

I believe that the truth will set me free (John 8:32) and that walking in the light is the only path of fellowship and freedom (1 John 1:7). Therefore, as a royal member of God's household, I stand against Satan's deceptions by affirming all the doctrines of the Faith and by taking every thought captive in obedience to Christ (2 Cor 10:5).

I declare that the Bible and the Church are the only authoritative standards for me (2 Tim 3:15, 16).

I choose to speak the truth in love (Eph 4:15).

I choose to present my body as an instrument of righteousness, a living and holy sacrifice, and thus I renew my mind daily by the living Word of God in order that I may prove that the will of God is good, acceptable, and perfect (Rom 6:13; 12:1, 2).

I ask my heavenly Father to fill me with His Holy Spirit (Eph 5:18), to lead me into all truth (John 16:13), and to empower my life that I may live above sin and not carry out the desires of the flesh (Gal 5:16). I crucify the flesh (Gal 5:24) and choose to walk by the Spirit.

In making all these affirmations, I renounce all selfish goals and choose the ultimate goal of love (1 Tim 1:5). I choose to obey the greatest commandment to love the Lord my God will all my heart, soul, and mind, and to love my neighbor as myself (Matt 22:37-39). Amen.

Step 6 — Worship, Pray, and Fast

Worship as a Church Family: One of Satan's favorite lies, apart from having us believe that he does not exist, or that he does exist and is more powerful than he truly is, is that since God is everywhere and we can worship Him anywhere and do not need the "community of believers ", the Church family.

Although it is true that God is everywhere and worshiping Him anywhere is wholesome and good, it is false to believe that the Church is unnecessary. Since the earliest days of Christianity, communities of believers gathered together on the *Lord's Day* (Sunday).

Scripture is very clear on the subject of Church attendance and on how our submission to its authority is not only good but required. The Church, its leaders and members, are the Mystical Body of Christ here on Earth. To disobey the teachings of the Church as it relates to faith and morals is to disobey the teachings of Christ. To not attend church is also disobedience to Christ.

Paul admonishes those who do not come to Church in Hebrews 10:19-25:

Therefore, brothers, since through the blood of Jesus we have confidence of entrance into the sanctuary by the new and living way he opened for us through the veil, that is, his flesh, and since we have "a great priest over the house of God," let us approach with a sincere heart and in absolute trust, with our hearts sprinkled clean from an evil conscience and our bodies washed in pure water. Let us hold unwaveringly to our confession that gives us hope, for he who made the promise is trustworthy. We must consider how to rouse one another to love and good works. We should not stay away from our assembly, as is the custom of some, but encourage one another, and this all the more as you see the day drawing near.

Hebrews 13:17

Obey your leaders and submit to them; for they are keeping watch over your souls, as men who will have to give account. Let them do this joyfully, and not sadly, for that would be of no advantage to you.

Worship and prayer together as a family, prayer meetings, adoration, and other corporate settings, and in the privacy of the family at home is critical in developing spiritual health for the family and each family member. Such family devotion forms the foundation for all that each family does away from home in the world of school, work, and society.

Prayer is so important both in the family context and individually. It is important not just because prayer is something a Christian ought to do, but because prayer is communication.

The more we depend on God, the closer He is to us and we are to Him. Aligning ourselves with God, communicating with Him at all times and in all situations and personal decisions will unite our hearts to His. A heart united to the Creator will overflow with graces and blessings.

Prayer and Spiritual Warfare: In addition, a healthy prayer life destroys strongholds that demons may have in our lives and in our hearts. Without prayer we cannot hope to be delivered from spiritual afflictions. It is no secret —prayer, worship, devotion, and living the Christ-Life in all that it entails is the formula not only for deliverance from spiritual afflictions, but for living the victorious life in Christ.

When dealing with spiritual afflictions, however, some special prayer considerations may be needed. Scripture states that there are certain demons that will only respond to prayer as well as fasting: *"But this kind does not go out except by prayer and fasting."* (Matthew 17:21). If fasting can defeat even the strongest of fallen angels, just how powerful is this sacrifice that we can make?

Spiritual warfare prayers are very effective in defeating the enemy and drawing our hearts closer to God.

Step 7 — Live the Faith and Remain Faithful

Along with all the advice and recommendations of the first six steps, our healing and deliverance cannot be complete unless we act upon our faith. Doing good works and charitable acts of love are a natural outflow of our faith and necessary to lead a good Christian life. It is not enough to believe. James asks and admonishes in James 2:19,20, 26:

Do you still think it's enough just to believe that there is one God? Well, even the demons believe this, and they tremble in terror! Fool! When will you ever learn that faith that does not result in good deeds is useless?

Just as the body is dead without a spirit, so also faith is dead without good deeds.

James calls a man a fool who does not act upon his faith in James 1:22-25:

Be doers of the word and not hearers only, deluding yourselves. For if anyone is a hearer of the Word and not a doer, he is like a man who looks at his own face in a mirror. He sees himself, then goes off and promptly forgets what he looks like. But the one who peers into the prefect law of freedom and perseveres, and is not a hearer who forgets but a doer who acts, such a one shall be blessed in what he does.

It is hard to live the Christ-Life, but we must try. We must not have a faith that is dead and useless. We must not be a fool and not practice our faith. We must, rather, live out our faith and persevere in the faith:

1 Corinthians 9:23-27

All this I do for the sake of the gospel, so that I too may have a share in it. Do you not know that the runners in the stadium all run in the race, but only one wins the prize? Run so as to win. Every athlete exercises discipline in every way. They do it to win a perishable crown, but we an imperishable one. Thus, I do not run aimlessly; I do not fight as if I were shadowboxing. No, I drive my body and train it, for fear that, after having preached to others, I myself should be disqualified.

Colossians 1:17-23

He is before all things, and in him all things hold together. He is the head of the body, the church. He is the beginning, the firstborn from the dead, that in all things he himself might be preeminent. For in him all the fullness was pleased to dwell, and through him to reconcile all things for him, making peace by the blood of his cross (through him), whether those on earth or those in heaven.

And you who once were alienated and hostile in mind because of evil deeds he has now reconciled in his fleshly body through his death, to present you holy, without blemish, and irreproachable before him, provided that you persevere in the faith, firmly grounded, stable, and not shifting from the hope of the gospel that you heard, which has been preached to every creature under heaven, of which I, Paul, am a minister.

And thus, let us be able to say, with St. Paul, in 2 Timothy 4:6-8

For I am already on the point of being sacrificed; the time of my departure has come. I have fought the good fight, I have finished the race, I have kept the faith. Henceforth there is laid up for me the crown of righteousness, which the Lord, the righteous judge, will award to me on that Day, and not only to me but also to all who have loved His appearing.

Persevere in the faith and let your life be a living Gospel for you shall thereby *"know the truth and the truth shall set you free"*

I have outlined steps detailing certain issues that we have found important in gaining freedom for a person in spiritual affliction.

1. purify one's conscience by a good confession;
2. Receive Holy Communion as often as possible;
3. Implore the mercy of God by prayer and fasting.
4. Recourse to specific spiritual warfare prayers applicable to the situation.

Final Thoughts

Repentance, forgiveness, acting on our faith, praying, fasting, receiving the Sacrament frequently, and all the rest we ought to do as good Christians are very good things and very necessary for this life, but more importantly for the life to come.

The advice contained in these Steps to Self-Deliverance, however, are not "quick fixes". This advice involves a lifelong commitment for anyone with spiritual afflictions. Freeing yourself from the bondages of the enemy and keeping them from returning requires this commitment to persevere in Christ and in the Christ-life.

There will be dry times. Your faith will be tested. Indeed, the demons may (and more than likely will) try to return. Scripture speaks of what demons do once they are cast out:

Now when the unclean spirit goes out of a man, it passes through waterless places seeking rest, and does not find it. Then it says, 'I will return to my house from which I came'; and when it comes, it finds it unoccupied, swept, and put in order. Then it goes and takes along with it seven other spirits more wicked than itself, and they go in and live there; and the last state of that man becomes worse than the first. (Matthew 12, 43-45).

Do not leave your house (heart) *"unoccupied, swept and put in order"*; rather be filled with the Holy Spirit.

We can never let down our guard. As a final instruction, remember the teaching of St. Paul in Ephesians 6:10-18. We do not go about our day without putting on our clothes. Do not go into the world with God's armor:

Finally, draw your strength from the Lord and from his mighty power. Put on the armor of God so that you may be able to stand firm against the tactics of the devil. For our struggle is not with flesh and blood but with the principalities, with the powers, with the world rulers of this present darkness, with the evil spirits in the heavens. Therefore, put on the armor of God that you may be able to resist on the evil day and, having done everything, to hold your ground. So, stand fast with your loins girded in truth, clothed with righteousness as a breastplate, and your feet shod in readiness for the gospel of peace. In all circumstances, hold faith as a shield, to quench all (the) flaming arrows of the evil one. And take the helmet of salvation and the sword of the Spirit, which is the word of God. With all prayer and supplication, pray at every opportunity in the Spirit. To that end, be watchful with all perseverance and supplication.

APENDEX 1
Steps for Self-Deliverance

The purpose of all this information is to enable you to do a self-deliverance at home for yourself. The process of self-deliverance is carried out in stages. Let's go through them one by one.

STEP ONE: Start with praise and worship. You can sing songs to praise God and to worship Him.

STEP TWO: Confess out loud Scriptures promising deliverance. Luke 10:19, Ephesians 1:7, Romans 16:20, Revelation 12:11, Colossians 2:14-15, Galatians 3:13-14, Psalms 91:3…*2 Timothy 4:18* says And the Lord shall deliver me from every evil work, and will preserve me unto His heavenly kingdom: to whom be glory forever and ever. Amen. You should memorize *2 Tim 4:18*.

STEP THREE: Break covenants and curses to destroy their legal hold. You pray a simple prayer like this: I break any curse or covenant working against me, in the name of Jesus. (Simple prayers)

STEP FOUR: Bind all the spirits associated with those covenants and curses like this: I bind all the spirits attached or connected to the curses and covenants I have just broken, in the name of Jesus.

STEP FIVE: Lay one hand on your head and pray, Holy Ghost, cover me from the top of my head to the sole of my feet, in the name of Jesus. Begin to mention every organ of your body; kidney, liver, intestine, blood, etc. You must not rush at this level. Lay your hands-on areas that the Spirit of God leads you to.

STEP SIX: Then begin to saturate yourself with the Blood of Jesus. You do this by saying: I plead the Blood of Jesus over me. This must continue until you have a release in your spirit to stop.

STEP SEVEN: It is now, that you can demand firmly, in the name of the Lord Jesus Christ, that any spirit that is not of God should leave you. You demand it forcefully like this: In the name of the Lord Jesus Christ, I come against all you hidden spirits and I bind your activities in my life. You can no longer hide below the surface because I now recognize what you have been doing; release me, in the name of Jesus.

(***If sickness is the problem, address it and say***) You spirit of infirmity, I speak to you directly, get out of my life now. I am redeemed by the Blood of Jesus Christ, come out and go now. Go out with every breath by the power of the Holy Spirit. I prevail over you, in the name of Jesus.

STEP EIGHT: Ask for a fresh in-filling of the Holy Spirit and close the session with praises. Self-deliverance keeps you from getting sick; it removes every evil seed of the enemy; it charges your body with fire. It uproots evil plantations and builds up your confidence. Every night before you go to bed, you must remember these two important prayer points.

1. Pray for cover with the Blood of Jesus. **_Revelation 12:11_** = And they overcame him by the Blood of the Lamb, and by the word of their testimony; and they loved not their lives unto the death.
2. Pray that the Angels of God should surround you. **_Psalms 34:7_** = The Angel of the Lord encampeth round about them that fear him, and delivereth them.

No matter how sleepy you are, make sure pray these two prayer points every night. There is no reason why self-deliverance should not be effective. However, if the person seeking deliverance is under stubborn demonic control or hereditary strongman and lacks sufficient faith or authority to defeat the oppressors or living in any known sin, the evil spirits will be hard to get rid of. right.

One final word of caution. For a person to be delivered, he/she must want deliverance. Self-deliverance must not be done because of pride, shyness, the fear of possible public embarrassment, etc. Your motive for engaging in self-deliverance has to be pure.

REMEMBER: **_DELIVERANCE IS A PROCESS (((NOT A ONE-TIME EVENT)))_** AND THE LENGTH OF TIME IT TAKES DEPENDS ON SEVERAL THINGS;

1. The length of time the spirit has stayed inside a person
2. The strength and reinforcement of the spirit
3. The experience and degree of anointing upon those who are ministering the deliverance
4. The willingness of the person being delivered to be free
5. The knowledge of the Word of God and your level of hatred for sin
6. SELF-DISCIPLINE IS NECESSARY

Also, remember that bondage can be weak or strong. A weak hold can be broken quickly, whereas a stronghold may take a more time. You will not realize the strength of bondage until you faithfully and persistently work on it. You must remember that a foothold can graduate to a stronghold if left unaddressed. After this exercise, set aside some days (with fasting). DO NOT CONTINUE TO DO THE THINGS THAT CAUSED THE "it"! CHANGE YOUR HABITS TO AGREE WITH YOUR PRAYERS. AMEN.

Appendix 2

Exposing the Doors to Bondage

Part I: The bondage

1. When did this bondage start?

2. Was there any unusual things that took place (or you did) when this bondage started?

3. If this bondage started when you were a child: Do you have ancestors who have suffered from a similar kind of bondage?

4. What kind of bondage are you facing? (Fears, depression, voices in your mind, mental illness, physical illness, mental torment, spiritual torment, etc. Please be as detailed as possible.)

5. What are all the things that have impacted your life? (Parent's death, trauma, a certain situation that changed your life, anything that 'changed' you.)

Part II: Your ancestor's background

1. Do you have ancestors who have struggled with similar problems or bondages?

2. Did your bondage start as a child and appear to have no reason to be there?

3. Do you have siblings who suffer from similar bondages or oppression?

Part III: Soul ties

1. Have you been involved with extramarital sex? Are you attracted to an ex-lover? Is he or she a good/godly influence for you?

2. Have you been divorced?

3. Do you feel an unusual attraction to a past boyfriend, girlfriend or lover (who is obviously not right for you)?

4. Do you let anybody dominate, control, or make your choices you?

5. Have you ever formed a blood covenant with another person? (Blood brothers, etc.)

6. Have you ever made vows or agreements with somebody in effort to strengthen the relationship or commit yourself to each other?

7. Do you see any ungodly relationships in your past where gifts were exchanged? (Are you holding onto something that was given to you from somebody you had adultery with, etc.)

8. Have you ever had ungodly relations with any one?

9. Do you have any pictures in your possession of somebody whom you may have an ungodly soul tie with? (A picture of you with somebody you had an adultery with, etc.)

Part IV: Relationship with parents

1. What do you think of your parents?

2. How would you explain your childhood?

3. Where you close to your parents while growing up? If not, why?

4. How would you explain your relationship with your parents? Was it good, bad or very cold?

5. Did you feel rejection from your parents?

6. Was either of your parents overly passive or controlling?

7. Has either of your parents been divorced? Remarried? Are your parents divorced?

8. How would you describe your relationship with your siblings growing up?

Part V: Rejection and abuse

1. Were your parents married when you were conceived? Were you the right sex? Did your parents not want you, or want you to be different (gender, etc.) in any way? If so, explain.

2. Did you feel rejected as a child? As an adult? If so, by whom? Explain.

3. Did you face abuse? What kind (emotional, physical, sexual, etc.) and by whom?

4. Have you faced rejection from your peers, classmates, friends or those around you?

5. Have you ever been put down, belittled, or made fun of? If so, by whom? Explain.

6. If you have faced rejection or abuse, how did you respond? Do you feel you are still paying a price for it? If so, how?

7. How do you respond to rejection right now?

8. Do you reject yourself (self-rejection)? If so, why and in what ways?

Part VI: Unforgiveness or bitterness

1. Is there anybody you feel edgy around? (Don't like them, feel anything in your heart against them, etc.)

2. Do you have anything against anybody? In other words, is there anybody that you have a hard time demonstrating the love of Christ to?

3. Has anybody wronged you that you haven't forgiven from your heart (thoughts, feelings, emotions, etc.)?

4. How do your view your siblings, parents, coworkers, etc.? Do you have any hard feelings against them?

5. Do you make a habit of blaming yourself for everything? Do you obsess over your mistakes and feel unusually guilty for them?

6. Do you deeply regret things that you've done in your past? Could you kick yourself over something you've done in your past? If so, explain.

Part VII: Personality

1. Are you a very positive or negative person?

2. Do you feel confident in yourself? If so, why?

3. Do you have a low self-esteem? If so, why?

4. Are you domineering or controlling? If so, to whom, and in what ways? Why?

5. Are you an achiever? (A go-getter) If so, in what ways?

6. Do you feel that you are always right and that if everybody did everything your way, this world would be a better place to live?

7. How do you treat your children? Husband? Are you controlling, passive, etc.?

8. Do you like people to 'look at you' (as in receive attention)?

Part VIII: Emotional health

1. Do you strive to feel accepted? If so, how does this affect your lifestyle? By whom do you want to feel accepted?

2. Are you always stressed out? If so, why?

3. Do you feel hurt? If so, by whom/what and why?

4. Do you feel good about yourself? If not, why?

5. Do you feel depressed? If so, why? When did it start? Did your parents or grandparents struggle with depression? If so, then do you know when it started and why? Do you have siblings who are also struggling? Do you feel your depression is rational or irrational?

6. Do you struggle with fears? If so, what is it that you fear? (Fear of heights, dying, being hopeless, failure, never marrying, etc.)

7. Do you worry about things? What things do you worry about? Why?

8. Do you struggle with anger? Do you have a short temper?

9. Do you have any insecurity? If so, explain.

10. Do you feel any self-pity or feel sorry for yourself? Have you ever felt this? If so, why?

11. Do you find it easy to hate people? If so, over what kinds of things would a person have to do to make you hate them?

12. Do you have any irrational feelings? If so, what are they?

13. Do you feel like something is wrong with you?

14. Do you feel excessively guilty over anything? Is this a continual problem?

15. Are you very confused and forgetful? (Beyond the normal)

16. Are you aware of any emotional wounds that have affected you?

17. Have you ever been deeply embarrassed over something? What was it?

18. Have you been in or are currently experiencing very difficult (depressing) circumstances which may cause you to feel hopeless or depressed?

Part IX: Who are you in Christ? And how do you see God?

1. How do you explain your relationship with God?

2. Do you feel you aren't good enough to meet His standards?

3. Do you see Him as a loving father, or a dictator?

4. Do you believe that it's only by the Blood of Jesus that your sins are forgiven? Or do you feel you need to earn your forgiveness in any way?

5. Do you feel God's love in your life?

6. Do you feel like your sins are forgiven? Or do you feel guilty?

7. Do you feel excessively guilty in everyday life?

8. Do you feel that doing good things, you earn God's love and acceptance?

9. Do you feel that God is angry or upset with you?

Part X: Spoken curses, vows & oaths

1. Have you ever spoken something negative about yourself that has come to past? For example: "I'm sick and tired..." or "If I don't quit typing, I'm going to get arthritis!"

2. Has your parents, or those in authority over you spoken out a curse over you? For example: "You'll never amount to anything!" or "You'll never get out of debt" or "You're so dumb"

3. Have you ever made a vow out of anger? If so, what? For example: "I'll never let anybody push me around again!" or "I'm never going to be hurt again!"

4. Have you ever wished to die? Have you ever said it?

5. If you have made any vows or oaths, what are they?

Part XI: Relationships

1. Do you have many friends? What kind of people are they?

2. Do you have a hard time trying to meet new people or make friends?

3. Are you socially outgoing or shy? If so, why?

4. How would you define your relationship with your spouse?

Part XII: Sexuality

1. Have you ever had unholy sex? What kind? (Fornication, adultery, sodomy, with a child, etc.)

2. Have you struggled with lust, fantasy or unholy sexual thoughts? If so, what kind?

3. Have you been attracted to pornography?

4. Do you have homosexual thoughts and desires? If so, have you acted upon those feelings?

5. How do you feel about your sexuality? (Do you feel dirty about it, or do you feel it's a wonderful blessing that God's given you?)

6. Do you withhold sex from your spouse or are you fidgety? Do you enjoy a healthy relationship with your spouse sexually? How does he or she react?

7. Have you ever been raped or sexually abused?

8. Have you ever woke up and felt a sexual presence with you? There are demons that imitate male and female functions, and stimulate their host (a person) sexually (beyond the normal 'wet dream').

9. Do you struggle or have you struggled with masturbation?

10. Do you struggle or have you struggled with any other sexual related thoughts, desires, or bondages?

11. Is there anything sexually that you are ashamed of?

Part XIII: Addictions

1. Do you have any addictions? If so, what kind? (Drugs, alcohol, smoking, eating, sex, TV, etc.) When did they start?

2. Did anybody else in your family (siblings, ancestors, etc.) have a struggle with any addictions? If so, what? Who?

3. Have you ever had, or currently have any sort of obsession over anything? If so, what?

Part XIV: False religions

Examples of false religions: Buddhism, Hindu, Jehovah Witness, Mormonism, Christian Scientists, eastern religions, etc.

1. Have you ever been involved with any false religions? If so, why, when and how long? How do you feel about those beliefs now?

2. Have you ever been involved in any secret societies such as Freemasonry? If so, how deep were you involved?

Part XV: The occult

1. Have you ever shown interest in the occult? If so, in what ways? (Read up on it, dabbled in it, etc.)

2. Do you still feel drawn or attracted to the occult?

3. Have you had any interest in horror or thriller style movies or novels? Are you still attracted to these things?

4. Have you ever made a vow with the devil? If so, what?

5. Married Satan?

6. Worshipped a demon or Satan?

7. Have you ever put a curse or spell on somebody?

8. Are you aware of any curses or spells placed on you? If so, what? Who did it?

9. Dabbled with an Ouija board? If so, why?

10. Ever been a member of a coven (group of 13 witches)? Explain.

11. Communicated with the dead? Explain.

12. Told somebody's fortune or went to see a fortune teller? Explain.

13. Ever read your horoscope?

14. Watched or been involved in a séance? Explain.

15. Have you been involved or a victim of Satanic Ritual Abuse (SRA)? Explain.

16. Been baptized into a false religion or any other evil baptism? If so, what were you baptized into? When?

17. Have you ever had a spirit guide?

18. Have you ever been involved with meditation, yoga, karate, or related activities?

19. Were you or anybody in your family superstitious? If so, who?

20. Ever been involved in astral travel? (Out of body)

21. If you have made any vows or oaths, what are they? Were there any sacrifices or rituals that were accompanied with them?

22. Have you ever made a blood pact before? If so, with whom (including persons, demons and Satan) and for what purpose?

23. Have you ever partaken in automatic writing, automatic drawing or automatic painting?

24. Have you ever been involved in Yoga, transcendental meditation, or similar activities?

25. Have you ever sought healing from a spiritual source other than Jesus Christ? (New age healing, energy healing, etc.)

26. Any other involvement in the occult? Explain.

Part XVI: Un-confessed sins

1. Are there any un-confessed sins that you have not repented of? (Usually something you've done, that you know is wrong, but won't admit to it. An abortion, stealing, etc. are some examples.)

2. Is there anything you've been hiding inside that you haven't confessed?

3. Do you feel excessively guilty over something(s) you've done in the past? If so, what?

Part XVII: Cursed objects

1. Do you have any idols, occult rings, or anything that could hold evil spiritual value in your home? If so, what? Any objects that hold evil spiritual value must be destroyed.

2. Do you have any gifts saved from sinful relationships? If so, explain. For example, if a man gives a woman a personal gift during an adultery that needs to be sold or destroyed.

Part XVIII: Severe trauma, abuse & disassociation

1. Have you ever been exposed to extreme abuse or a traumatic experience? Did it have a drastic effect on your emotional or mental system? If so, what happen? How did it affect you?

2. Have you ever disassociated or been diagnosed with Dissociative Identity Disorder (DID) or Multiple Personality Disorder (MPD)?

3. Are you aware of any alters (other personalities) that you may have? (If so, tell me about them)

4. Do you have a memory gap where you cannot remember a certain time of your life?

5. Do you have false memories of things that really didn't take place?

6. Have you ever been in a car accident or other traumatic situation? Have you ever witnessed a tragedy in real life?

Part XIX: Weaknesses

1. Do you struggle with any habitual sins? If so, what? Do you want to break those bad habits?

2. Do you struggle with any weaknesses such as lust, anger, hate, etc.? If so, what? Do you know where they came from or how they got started? Do you want to break free from those weaknesses?

Part XX: Pregnancy issues

1. Have you ever said something along the lines of, "I will never have children"?

2. Have you ever had an abortion or attempted one?

3. Have you ever had incest or ungodly sexual relations with somebody related to you? (See Leviticus 20:19-21, as this can cause a curse to land upon you which needs to be broken)

Part XXI: Other things to look for

1. Have you ever tried drugs? If so, how much, and how did it affect you? Why did you try drugs?

2. Have you ever thought about or attempted suicide?

3. Do you have any physical or mental disabilities, diseases or illnesses? Explain.

4. Do you want, and are willing to be delivered? Are you willing to give up those demon spirits and maybe make some lifestyle changes in order to keep your deliverance?

5. Do you experience unusual confusion settle upon you as you try to pray and read the Bible?

6. What kind of music do you like? (Please list all styles of music you currently enjoy, and give examples in each category you list, such as some names of artists and songs)

7. Have you previously enjoyed hard rock, metal, acid, alternative, rap, new age, or any other kind of worldly music? (Please provide some examples of artists and songs from each genre (type/style) of music you list)

8. Have you had any nightmares or weird experiences at night while supposedly sleeping?

9. Have you ever been in a trance or had an out of body experience?

10. Have you ever noticed time slipped right out from under you? For example, you look at your watch and its 7:00pm, then you look again what seemed like 15 minutes later and its 2:00am. This is a sign of a trance.

11. Have you ever touched or kissed a dead body? If so, explain whom and why and what happened afterwards.

12. Do you feel that you somehow have to earn your forgiveness? Do you 'wonder' if your sins are truly forgiven -- all of them? Are you aware of any signs of legalism or religious spirits operating in your mind?

13. Do you have any physical infirmities, sickness or diseases? If so, please list them.

14. Are you on any medications? If so, please explain.

15. Are you entertained by movies or TV shows which glorify death, murder, pain or suffering of others? Please explain.

16. Have you ever had any other kind of weird encounter with the spiritual realm?

Use this information to expose the root cause of the "it".

REFERENCES

1. Gary R. Collins, *Christian Counseling: A Comprehensive Guide*, 3rd Addition, Revised and Updated, NavPress, Colorado Springs, Colorado. ISBN 1418503290
2. Beilby, J.K. & P.R. Eddy. *Understanding Spiritual Warfare: Four Views*. Grand Rapids, Michigan: Baker, 2012.
3. Boyd, G.A., *God at War: The Bible and Spiritual Conflict*. Downers Grove, Illinois: IVP, 1997.
4. Hiebert, P. "Spiritual Warfare and Worldview"
5. Stedman, R.C, *Spiritual Warfare: Winning the Daily Battle with Satan.* Portland, Oregon: Multnomah, 1975.
6. Pirolo, N., *Prepare for Battle: Basic Training in Spiritual Warfare*, San Diego, California: Emmaus Road, International, 1997.
7. Arnold, E. C., *3 Crucial Questions about Spiritual Warfare*, Grand Rapids, Michigan: Baker, 1997.l
8. Rita Bennett, You Can Be Emotionally Free, 1982 ISBN 978 0 88270 748 8
9. Rita Bennett, Emotionally Free, 1982, ISBN 0 86065 194 0
   Publishers, PO Box 777,
10. Tonbridge, Kent TN 11 0ZS, England, 1997, reprinted 2004). ISBN 1-85240-110-9. (Available in the US through the Arsenal Bookstore, 11005 Voyager Parkway, Colorado Springs, CO 80921.)
11. John and Paula Sandford, Healing the Wounded Spirit (Victory House, 1985). ISBN 0-932081-14-2.
12. Norma Dearing, The Healing Touch (Chosen Books, 2002). ISBN 0-8007-9302-1. Charles Kraft, Deep Wounds, Deep Healing (Servant Pub., 1993). ISBN 0-89283-784-5.
13. Derek Prince, God's Remedy for Rejection (Whitaker House, 1993). ISBN 088368-864-6.
14. Francis and Judith MacNutt, Praying for Your Unborn Child (1989). ISBN 0-38523-2829. (Available from www.Christianhealingmin.org, 904-765-3332.)
15. Thomas Verney, MD, The Secret Life of the Unborn Child (Summit Books, 1981).
16. Anderson, Winning Spiritual Warfare 1990 ISBN 13: 978-0-89081-868-8 James
17. Friesen, Uncovering the Mystery of MPD, 1997 ISBN 1-56819-062-7
18. Diane Hawkins, Multiple Identities, 2009 ISBN 978-0-9708073-6-6,
19. Restoration in Christ Ministries, http://www.rcm-usa.org/index.htm
20. Francis MacNutt, Deliverance from Evil Spirits, 1995, 0-8007-9232-7, Chap 17, pp 223-235 (best introductory material)
21. Daniel Ryder, Breaking the Circle of SRA, 1992, 0-89638-258-3 (an excellent book by a Christian counselor)
22. Margaret Smith, Ritual Abuse, what it is, why it happens, how to help, 1993, 0-06-250214-X (in depth information about SRA and MPD)
23. The Christian Bible
24. The following associations focus on trauma and disassociation www.sidran.org, www.issd.org
25. Pentecost, J.D., *Your Adversary the Devil.* Grand Rapids, Michigan: Zondervan, 1969

About the Author
Dr. Paulette Douglas

Dr. Paulette Douglas truly epitomizes elegance in living a saved, sanctified and Holy life, set apart from the secular world! Dr. Douglas is an ordained minister with the Pentecostal Assemblies of the World, an anointed national and international Evangelist, teacher and preacher. Dr. Paulette Douglas is renowned for the ministry of exhortation to the Body of Christ through deliverance, inner healing, salvation and biblical counseling at seminars, prayer clinics, crusades and conferences. She has established three churches and assisted in establishing many other churches, ministries and colleges as she serves on the Body of Christ for Jesus. Dr. Douglas was baptized in the name of Jesus Christ and filled with the Holy Ghost in 1977. She was called to the ministry in 1981, taught bible study at Pacific Bell for nine years which established the Radiant Life in Christ Ministries. She was the founder and pastor of the Radiant Life in Christ Community Church in Baldwin Park, California for nearly four years. Dr. Douglas retired in 1996 with full benefits from AT&T after 26 years of service. God introduced Dr. Douglas to the LOVE and HERO of her life, Bishop Robert T. Douglas Sr. They were married, the ministries merged, and she became the First Lady of the Jacob's Ladder Family, the Women's Ministry Director, the Church Executive Administrator and the Dean of the California University of Theology. Dr. Robert and Paulette Douglas are the proud parents of three wonderful children, Shakinah, Robert Jr. and Sondra Imani. They are also blessed with two granddaughters, Demi and Rob'Ann (butter ball) four grandsons, Dylan, Dominick Terrell, the twins Canden and Caden. Seven Godchildren and twelve God -grandchildren. Dr. Douglas is a graduate from Fuller Theological Seminary, Pasadena, California, Pentecostal Bible College, Ministerial Training Institute of Inglewood, California and Aenon Bible College West Coast. She has a Bachelors degree in Biblical Studies, a Masters degree in Theology, a PhD in Theology, Administration and a PhD in Biblical Counseling. She has earned certificates from California Christian Leadership of Orange County in biblical counseling, Zoe Christian Leadership Training Institute, Church Growth International, Seoul Korea and School of World Missions and Evangelism, Los Angeles. Dr. Douglas is formerly the Dean/Professor of the Inglewood Ministerial Training Institute of Inglewood, the Inland Empire Ministerial Training Institute, the Tri-County Ministerial Training Institute (San Bernardino, Riverside and Los Angeles counties) and the Living Waters Bible College, Rialto California. Dr. Douglas is presently the Dean of Colleges and Professor for the California District Council Aenon Bible College and Institutes, the Jacob's Ladder California University of Theology and Aenon Bible Institute CDC Extension Campus in Inglewood, California and the American College Theological Seminary International University (ACTS). All schools are fully accredited institutions for pastors, evangelist, teachers and anyone who has the call of God on their lives for ministry. Dr. Douglas is currently the CDC International Missions President and the past Church/Extension/Evangelism/Altar Director for the California District Council of the Pentecostal Assemblies of the World, Inc. Past Evangelism President for the CHDC Area 2 and has worked with the PAW Evangelism Ministry for more than 35 years. Dr. Paulette Douglas is the published author of the book series "Get Rid of It before It Gets Rid of You". Self-Help Instructions on how to correct and receive deliverance in every area of your life. Dr. Douglas portrays tremendous strength and endurance in the Lord by jointly sharing the vision and love for God with Bishop Douglas. Her primary objective in life is to be that "Excellent Woman of God, walking in His Divine favor.

Books and Recourses Compiled by
Dr. Paulette Douglas

"How to Get Rid of "it", Before "it" Gets Rid of You" Series (12 Books on Self Deliverance)

Volume One- Healing and Deliverance from Additions

Volume Two- Healing and Deliverance from Sexual Additions

Volume Three- Healing and Deliverance from Personality Disorders

Volume Four- Healing and Deliverance from Negative Relationships

Volume Five- Healing and Deliverance Through Spiritual Warfare

Volume Six- Healing and Deliverance from Negatives Attitudes

Volume Seven- Healing and Deliverance from Success Hindrances

Volume Eight- Healing and Deliverance from Tormenting Emotions

Volume Nine- Healing and Deliverance from Spiritual Weakness

Volume Ten- Healing and Deliverance from Salvation Issues

Volume Eleven- Healing and Deliverance from Domestic Problems

Volume Twelve- Healing and Deliverance Through Biblical Counseling

How to Have an Anointed Altar Workers Ministry

How to Have an Effective Prayer and Fasting Life

How to Walk in Your Grace as the Wife of a Minister, Deacon, Pastor, or Bishop

How to be an Effective Life Coach